The Quiet Climb

How Introverts Build Powerful Businesses, How to Lead,

Sell, and Succeed Without Shouting

Nicci Brochard
&
Dr. Ben Chuba

The Quiet Climb

How Introverts Build Powerful Businesses, How to Lead,

Sell, and Succeed Without Shouting

Book Formatting by: Monisha

Book cover design by: *Billy Design*

CROSSBORDER

New York, London, Quebec

Contents

Introduction..1

    The Quiet Climb – How Introverts Build Powerful Businesses.............................1
    What Makes This Book Different...2
    A New Approach to Leadership..3
    Selling with Subtle Power..3
    Succeeding on Your Own Terms...4
    A New Definition of Success...4

PART I: DESIGNING A BUSINESS THAT FITS YOU 1

Chapter 1: The Myth of the Loud Leader.......................................2

    Introduction: The Prevailing Culture of Extroversion in Business.....................2
    1. Why Extroversion Is Overrated in Business Culture 3
    The Business World's Obsession with Extroversion...................................3
    The Illusion of Extroversion as Confidence 4
    2. Quiet Isn't Weak: Understanding the Misjudgment of Silence 5
    The Power of Reflection and Listening...5
    The Quiet Leader's Strategic Advantage 5
    3. Real-Life Examples of Quiet Leadership Success 6
    Warren Buffett: The Ultimate Introverted Leader 6
    Bill Gates: The Silent Innovator...7
    4. Shifting the Narrative: Quiet Leadership as a Strength............................7
    The Case for Quiet Leadership..7
    The Future of Leadership..8
    Conclusion: A New Era of Leadership..8

Chapter 2: The Introvert Advantage 10

    Introduction: The Hidden Power of Introversion in Business 10
    1. Traits That Make Introverts Exceptional Entrepreneurs.........................11
    The Power of Deep Thinking and Reflection 11
    Focused Work: Embracing the Power of Solitude....................................12
    Creativity and Innovation in Solitude..12
    2. High Empathy and Emotional Intelligence..13
    The Introvert's Superpower: Empathy...13
    Building Strong, Trust-Based Relationships..14

3. Comparing Quiet Power with Loud Charisma.....................................15

The Loud Charisma Trap 15

The Quiet Leader's Impact..16

Quiet Leadership and the Modern Business World 16

Conclusion: Harnessing the Introvert Advantage..................................16

Chapter 3: Building Confidence Without Performing 18

Introduction: The Quiet Confidence of Authentic Leadership..............18

1. Developing Internal Validation Over External Applause 19

The Need for External Validation in a Performance-Driven World 19

What is Internal Validation? 20

2. How to Show Up Authentically Without Faking Extroversion 21

The Pressure to Perform..21

Embrace Your Unique Strengths...22

Embrace Quiet Leadership..23

3. Grounding Routines and Rituals to Reduce Social Exhaustion 24

Social Exhaustion: Understanding the Toll on Introverts.......................24

Establishing Grounding Rituals..24

Conclusion: Quiet Confidence, Bold Leadership 25

PART II: DESIGNING A BUSINESS THAT FITS YOU 27

Chapter 4: Quiet Branding – Attract Without the Hype 28

Introduction: The Power of Quiet Branding..28

1. Personal Branding for Introverts: Clarity Over Charisma..................29

The Challenge of Traditional Branding 29

Defining Your Brand with Purpose...30

2. How to Tell Your Story in a Subtle, Magnetic Way 31

The Power of Storytelling for Introverts..31

Crafting Your Narrative...32

3. Creating Content That Reflects Your Energy 33

The Difference Between "Loud" Content and "Quiet" Content.............33

How to Create Content That Feels Authentic...34

Conclusion: Quiet Branding as a Powerful Strategy..............................35

Chapter 5: Selling Without the Sleaze 36

Introduction: Redefining Sales with Integrity...36

1. Gentle Sales Strategies that Align with Your Values...........................37

The Shift Toward Authentic Sales..37

Empathy-Driven Sales...39

2. Building Trust Through Listening and Thoughtful Offers 40
Listening as the Foundation of Trust 40
Crafting Thoughtful Offers 41
3. Email Funnels, Webinars, and Soft-Sell Techniques.......................41
Email Funnels: Nurturing Relationships Without the Push...............41
Webinars: Providing Value Through Live Engagement.......................42
Soft-Sell Techniques: Selling Through Subtlety..................................43
Conclusion: Authentic Sales as a Path to Sustainable Success 43

Chapter 6: Building Systems to Speak for You 45

Introduction: The Power of Behind-the-Scenes Systems for Introverts.................45
1. Automations, Evergreen Content, and Systems That Reduce "Live" Energy Drains...46
The Necessity of Automating Repetitive Tasks 46
Using Evergreen Content for Long-Term Impact................................47
Customer Service Automations and CRM Tools.................................48
2. Creating Processes That Scale Quietly...49
The Importance of Process Building..49
Building a Team That Runs the Systems 50
3. Letting Your Backend Do the Heavy Lifting 51
Streamlining Your Backend for Efficiency...51
Integrating Tools for Maximum Impact..52
Conclusion: The Quiet Power of Systematic Success 52

PART III: LEADING WITHOUT SHOUTING..........54

Chapter 7: Silent Leadership in Action............................ 55

Introduction: The Strength of Silent Leadership.................................55
1. Redefining Leadership Through Presence and Consistency 56
The Power of Presence in Leadership 56
Consistency as a Pillar of Silent Leadership...57
2. Creating Psychological Safety for Your Team or Collaborators 58
What is Psychological Safety?..58
How Introverts Create Psychological Safety 59
3. Making Decisions with Calm Authority 61
The Calm Authority of Quiet Leaders...61
How to Make Decisions with Calm Authority.....................................61
Conclusion: Leading with Quiet Strength 62

Chapter 8: Managing Energy, Not Just Time 64

Introduction: The Hidden Power of Energy Management..........................64
1. Energy Management Strategies for Deep Work and Creative Focus..................65
The Importance of Deep Work..65
Maximizing Deep Work Through Energy Awareness 66
2. Designing Your Workweek to Prevent Burnout..................................67
Understanding the Energy Drains of a Typical Workweek.......................67
Creating a Balanced Workweek for Introverts.....................................68
3. Social Recovery Time: Why It's Not a Luxury..................................70
The Importance of Social Recovery for Introverts.................................70
Creating a Social Recovery Plan..70
Conclusion: Mastering Energy for Sustainable Success 71

Chapter 9: Networking for the Quiet Soul 73

Introduction: The Quiet Power of Meaningful Connections.......................73
1. How to Build a Meaningful Network Without Constant Small Talk.................74
The Dread of Small Talk 74
Strategic Networking vs. Networking for the Sake of It............................74
Building Relationships Through Shared Values 75
2. Strategic Online Networking 77
Leveraging Social Media for Introverts 77
The Power of Authentic Online Connections...78
3. Thoughtful Relationship-Building Over Hustle 79
The Cost of the Hustle Culture 79
Building Meaningful Relationships Over Time.......................................79
Conclusion: Quiet Networking as a Strength...80

PART IV: SCALING WITH EASE AND INTEGRITY 82

Chapter 10: Thought Leadership, the Introvert Way.................... 83

Introduction: The Quiet Power of Thought Leadership.............................83
1. Becoming a Go-To Expert Without Shouting 84
What is Thought Leadership?...84
Leading with Quiet Authority...86
2. Blogging, Podcasting, and Long-Form Content as Tools of Influence 87
Blogging: The Power of Written Thought Leadership..............................87
Podcasting: Voice as a Tool for Thought Leadership 88
3. The Compound Effect of Consistent Quiet Thought Leadership..................90
Consistency is Key..90
Building a Legacy of Quiet Influence...90
Conclusion: Quiet Thought Leadership as a Lasting Influence 91

Chapter 11: Building a Loyal Audience Without the Spotlight..... 92

Introduction: The Power of Quiet Influence..92
1. Cultivating a Small-but-Mighty Community.................................93
The Value of Smaller, More Focused Communities 93
2. Leveraging Authenticity and Resonance Over Reach 95
Authenticity as the Core of Connection...95
3. Engagement Without Constant Presence......................................97
The Challenge of Constant Availability...97
Creating Consistent, Value-Driven Content....................................97
The Power of Scheduling "Social Recovery" Time.........................98
Conclusion: Building a Legacy of Quiet Influence.........................98

Chapter 12: Collaborating Without Losing Yourself 100

Introduction: The Art of Collaboration for Introverts 100
1. Partnering with Extroverts, Influencers, or Media Without Draining Your Energy...101
The Power of Introvert-Extrovert Partnerships 101
Key Strategies for Introverts in Collaborative Partnerships..................102
2. Setting Boundaries and Preserving Your Work Style 103
Why Boundaries Matter...103
Practical Tips for Setting Boundaries in Collaboration 104
3. Knowing When to Say No to "Big Opportunities" 105
The Temptation of "Big Opportunities".......................................105
How to Evaluate Opportunities and Know When to Say No 106
Conclusion: Embracing Collaborative Success Without Sacrificing Yourself........107

PART V: THE INNER WORK OF THE QUIET CLIMB 108

Chapter 13: Rewriting the Narrative – From "Too Quiet" to Powerful 109

Introduction: The Power of Quiet Strength...109
1. Reframing Past Feedback or Trauma Around Your Personality.....................110
The Weight of External Expectations...110
Recognizing the Origin of the Narrative.......................................111
2. Healing the Pressure to Be "More Outgoing"..............................112
The Myth of the Outgoing Leader 112
Healing from the Pressure...113
3. Reclaiming Quiet Confidence...114
What is Quiet Confidence?..114

How to Reclaim Quiet Confidence 114

Conclusion: Embracing Quiet Power..116

Chapter 14: Creating Success on Your Terms...............117

Introduction: Reclaiming Success..117

1. Defining Your Own Metrics of Success..118

The Problem with Society's Standard Metrics of Success.......................................118

Redefining Success as a Personal Journey 119

2. Case Examples of Quiet Businesses Thriving in Niche Ways............................120

Quiet Businesses Making a Big Impact 120

The Power of Consistency Over Flashy Visibility...121

3. Letting Go of Comparison and Visibility Pressure..122

The Dangers of Comparison Culture..122

Embracing Your Own Pace...122

Conclusion: Crafting Your Own Quiet Success...123

Chapter 15: The Quiet Climb Continues.......................125

Introduction: The Journey of Quiet Leadership...125

1. Sustaining Your Energy, Values, and Focus Over the Long Term....................126

The Importance of Self-Care for Introverted Entrepreneurs 126

Staying True to Your Values as You Grow...127

2. Evolving Your Business While Honoring Your Introversion............................129

Adapting Without Losing Your Authenticity..129

3. The Legacy of Silent Leadership...131

Building a Legacy Through Quiet Leadership...131

How to Build a Legacy of Silent Leadership 131

Conclusion: Quietly Climbing to Lasting Success...133

Epilogue 134

The Quiet Climb – Leading with Purpose, Power, and Authenticity.....................134

Introduction

The Quiet Climb – How Introverts Build Powerful Businesses

Society often celebrates loud personalities, extroverted traits, and constant networking, it's easy to believe that success in business requires the ability to speak loudly and dominate the spotlight. Yet, there's an emerging shift that highlights the power of those who thrive in quieter, introspective spaces—introverts. As more individuals and companies recognize the strengths that introverts bring to the table, the narrative around leadership, entrepreneurship, and success is evolving.

The quiet ones are often overlooked or underestimated in an environment that emphasizes extroversion. But the truth is, introverts are natural-born leaders, innovative thinkers, and extraordinary business builders. They might not be the loudest voice in the room, but their **deep** thinking, emotional intelligence, and methodical approach to problem-solving make them uniquely positioned to build lasting, sustainable businesses. The Quiet Climb is an exploration of how introverts can leverage their inner strengths to lead, sell, and succeed in business—without feeling the pressure to change their natural dispositions or engage in the typical "louder" ways of doing business.

This book aims to show introverts that they don't need to follow the traditional loud, gregarious mold of entrepreneurship to succeed.

Introverts have their own powerful way of moving through the world—one that relies on deep listening, thoughtful analysis, empathy, and building meaningful relationships. These are the very qualities that enable introverts to cultivate strong businesses that are built on trust, authenticity, and genuine connection.

As we venture through these pages, we'll explore how introverts can build businesses that are aligned with their strengths, while also embracing strategies that allow them to excel in areas that might feel challenging—like leadership, marketing, and sales. The goal is not to change who you are but to find ways to amplify your voice and impact without having to shout. The Quiet Climb is about discovering how introverts can thrive in business, not by pretending to be someone they're not, but by embracing who they truly are.

What Makes This Book Different

Unlike other business books that preach the importance of extroversion, this book takes a refreshing approach by celebrating the qualities that introverts naturally possess. Quiet leadership, introspection, strategic thinking, and emotional depth are all essential skills that introverts bring to their businesses. Through these lenses, introverts can create authentic brands, build strong teams, and nurture long-lasting customer relationships without resorting to traditional, loud marketing tactics.

Through actionable insights, real-life stories, and practical advice, this book will guide introverts through the various phases of building a successful business. From crafting a brand that aligns with your personality to navigating the world of sales with a quiet yet powerful approach, you will learn how to use your natural gifts to succeed.

A New Approach to Leadership

Introverts often shine when given the opportunity to lead in their own unique way. Rather than relying on grandiose gestures or charismatic speeches, introverts can lead with humility, empathy, and vision. They excel at one-on-one communication, listening deeply, and making decisions based on careful consideration. These qualities help introverted leaders build strong, loyal teams and create work environments where people feel valued, heard, and supported.

In this book, we'll dive into the nuances of introverted leadership, exploring how to inspire your team without resorting to traditional extroverted tactics. We'll look at quiet leadership strategies that empower introverts to lead with confidence and authenticity, while still maintaining their natural inclination for thoughtful reflection and deep connection.

Selling with Subtle Power

Selling can be one of the most intimidating aspects of running a business for introverts. The idea of "selling yourself" or your product in an aggressive, high-energy way may seem daunting. However, introverts are naturally skilled at building relationships—an essential component of successful sales. Rather than relying on loud sales pitches, introverts can use their strengths to engage in authentic conversations, listen attentively to customer needs, and craft offers that truly resonate. In this book, we'll explore how introverts can approach sales with subtle power and confidence, creating win-win situations for both themselves and their customers.

Succeeding on Your Own Terms

At the heart of The Quiet Climb is the idea that success is not one-size-fits-all. It is not about emulating extroverted styles of business but finding your own unique path—one that aligns with your personality, values, and skills. Introverts thrive in environments where they can slow down, reflect, and create businesses that have depth and meaning. This book is an invitation to build your business on your terms, embracing your quiet strengths as tools for lasting success.

By the end of this journey, you will have a clearer understanding of how to leverage your introverted nature to lead with authenticity, sell with integrity, and build a business that reflects who you are—all while staying true to your values and vision.

A New Definition of Success

The Quiet Climb is about success on your own terms, redefining what it means to thrive as an introvert in business. It's about moving away from the belief that you need to be loud, aggressive, or outgoing to succeed. Instead, you will learn that true success comes from building meaningful relationships, creating value, and leading with purpose.

This book is an invitation to embrace the power of quiet leadership—to recognize that your strengths, when fully understood and harnessed, can create incredible success and fulfillment. No longer should introverts feel they need to change to fit a certain mold; instead, they can rise and shine by being true to who they are.

Nicci and I (Ben) thank you for choosing our book. We promise you a great time ahead.

PART I

DESIGNING A BUSINESS THAT FITS YOU

Chapter 1

The Myth of the Loud Leader

Introduction: The Prevailing Culture of Extroversion in Business

In today's business world, success is often linked with being vocal, outgoing, and extroverted. We live in a culture that values loudness—whether it's in boardrooms, during meetings, or in social networks. Extroverted leaders are often perceived as confident, dynamic, and assertive—traits that are traditionally associated with effective leadership. But is being extroverted truly the defining trait of a great leader? And what about those who lead with a quieter, more introspective approach?

This chapter challenges the myth of the loud leader, arguing that extroversion is overrated in business culture, and quiet leadership should be recognized as equally powerful and effective. It delves into the misjudgments faced by those who lead with a quieter, more reserved style and offers a case for why silence and reflection should be seen as assets, not weaknesses. We will explore why the modern workplace needs to reconsider traditional views on leadership and how introverts—who make up a significant portion of the workforce—can thrive as leaders.

1. Why Extroversion Is Overrated in Business Culture

The Business World's Obsession with Extroversion

In traditional business settings, extroverts often dominate the narrative. The archetype of the charismatic, outspoken CEO or the talkative salesperson is perpetuated in media, corporate offices, and even in entrepreneurship. Extroversion is seen as a sign of strength—the louder, more visible a leader, the more likely they are to be celebrated. There's an implicit belief that extroverts have the confidence and social prowess necessary to build networks, inspire teams, and drive business success. But these assumptions come at the expense of quiet leaders who might not fit the standard mold but excel in ways that are less immediately visible.

Business culture has long placed a premium on qualities like assertiveness, outgoingness, and the ability to "command a room." But does this mean that these traits are truly necessary for leadership success? Is extroversion the only trait that makes one an effective leader, or is there a need to acknowledge the quiet strengths that introverts bring to the table?

The truth is, many highly successful leaders are introverts who have learned how to harness their natural tendencies to drive results without needing to be the loudest in the room. Yet, too often, their contributions go unnoticed or are undervalued because of a prevailing bias toward extroverted qualities. The preference for extroversion in business stems from long-standing cultural norms and the belief that success requires being outspoken, forceful, and outgoing—qualities that do not align with the more reserved, reflective tendencies that introverts bring.

The Illusion of Extroversion as Confidence

One of the key reasons why extroversion is often overrated is the mistaken link between being extroverted and being confident. While extroverts may appear to be more confident in social settings, this is not necessarily the case. Extroverts might speak more easily in front of a crowd, but this doesn't equate to true leadership. Confidence is not just about being loud; it is about having a deep understanding of your strengths and using them to support your team, make informed decisions, and create a lasting impact. Introverted leaders, with their reflective nature, often possess a different, yet equally valuable form of confidence—one that is self-aware, thoughtful, and grounded in strategic decision-making.

In fact, quiet leaders often exhibit greater emotional intelligence, which is a key factor in successful leadership. Their ability to listen actively, observe carefully, and approach challenges with patience makes them exceptional at solving problems and leading by example. Emotional intelligence—the ability to recognize, understand, and manage one's own emotions and the emotions of others—is arguably more important for leadership success than being able to give an impromptu speech or network with hundreds of people.

2. Quiet Isn't Weak: Understanding the Misjudgment of Silence

The Power of Reflection and Listening

In the fast-paced, high-pressure world of business, there is often a tendency to value action over contemplation. Silence is often misunderstood as a lack of contribution, as though a quiet leader is disengaged or disconnected from the conversation. But the truth is, the power of silence lies in the opportunity it provides for reflection and active listening. Introverted leaders, by nature, spend more time thinking and processing information before speaking. This careful approach leads to more considered decisions and an ability to evaluate situations from multiple angles. They tend to make decisions based on long-term strategy rather than reacting impulsively to immediate situations.

Listening is one of the most powerful tools a leader can possess, yet it's often overlooked in favor of speaking. Introverted leaders often excel in this area, taking time to listen and truly understand their employees' needs, thoughts, and concerns. This empathetic leadership style fosters trust and respect, and creates an environment where team members feel valued and understood. Active listening creates a culture of open communication, collaboration, and mutual respect within a team— qualities that are essential for success in any organization.

The Quiet Leader's Strategic Advantage

In contrast to the extroverted leader who may dominate conversations and make quick decisions, the quiet leader excels at strategic thinking. Introverts tend to think before they speak, carefully weighing all possible outcomes and considering the consequences of their decisions. While extroverts may rely on quick action, introverts rely on deliberation and strategy.

This ability to step back and assess the bigger picture gives introverted leaders a distinct advantage in the long term. They are not easily swayed by short-term pressures or external opinions, which allows them to make decisions that align with the company's long-term vision and values. By not rushing to offer immediate solutions, they create space for innovation, creativity, and more thoughtful problem-solving.

3. Real-Life Examples of Quiet Leadership Success

Warren Buffett: The Ultimate Introverted Leader

One of the most famous examples of a successful introverted leader is Warren Buffett, one of the world's wealthiest individuals and an iconic figure in the business world. Buffett is known for his quiet demeanor, thoughtful approach to investing, and ability to remain calm under pressure. His success is a testament to the fact that introverted qualities, such as patience, deep thinking, and careful decision-making, can lead to extraordinary achievements.

Buffett's success in business has never been about loud pitches or aggressive tactics. Instead, his focus has been on long-term investments, relationship-building, and a methodical approach to business. His ability to listen, observe, and take a step back before making major decisions has been a driving force in his success.

Bill Gates: The Silent Innovator

Another prime example of introverted leadership is Bill Gates, the co-founder of Microsoft. Gates has often been described as someone who prefers deep, focused work over attending high-profile events or making public appearances. His introverted nature was evident early on, as he spent countless hours programming, solving complex problems, and fine-tuning the company's software. Gates' ability to remain focused on the big picture while avoiding distractions has played a major role in his company's success.

Gates also demonstrated an ability to adapt his leadership style over time, becoming more of a public figure as Microsoft grew. However, his success has always been rooted in his ability to listen, analyze, and make decisions based on a deep understanding of the technology landscape.

4. Shifting the Narrative: Quiet Leadership as a Strength

The Case for Quiet Leadership

Quiet leadership is about embracing a leadership style that is authentic, thoughtful, and rooted in deep understanding. Introverts, when given the space to lead on their own terms, create environments that foster respect, collaboration, and meaningful connections. Their ability to listen, reflect, and think strategically makes them not just capable leaders, but exceptional ones.

In business culture, it's time to redefine leadership. Extroverted traits like loudness and assertiveness are no longer the sole indicators of success. It's time to recognize the quiet leaders who may not be as visible or vocal, but who shape organizations with their insightful decisions, emotional intelligence, and long-term vision. Quiet leadership is an invitation to lead with authenticity and purpose, embracing your true self without the need to conform to external expectations.

The Future of Leadership

The future of leadership lies in the balance of extroverted and introverted qualities. A truly effective leader is someone who can adapt, who understands when to speak and when to listen, and who knows how to create spaces for others to contribute their ideas and perspectives. As businesses continue to evolve, we'll see more and more organizations embracing the strengths of introverted leaders, fostering an environment that values depth over noise, reflection over reaction, and strategy over speed.

Conclusion: A New Era of Leadership

As the world of business continues to evolve, it's time to acknowledge that leadership comes in many forms. Extroversion is no longer the sole indicator of success. Quiet leaders, with their ability to think deeply, listen attentively, and make thoughtful decisions, are poised to thrive in the modern business world. By embracing the power of silence, introverts can rewrite the narrative of what it means to be a leader. The myth of the loud leader is being dismantled, and in its place, a new model of leadership is emerging—one that celebrates authenticity, thoughtfulness, and empathy. It's time for introverts to step into their true power and lead with confidence, knowing that their quiet strength is exactly what the business world needs.

Chapter 2

The Introvert Advantage

Introduction: The Hidden Power of Introversion in Business

In the modern world of business, where extroversion is often equated with leadership and success, introverts can sometimes feel overlooked or underappreciated. The business world often champions loud, charismatic leaders who thrive in social settings and public speaking. However, introverts possess a unique set of **traits** and abilities that make them not just capable but exceptional entrepreneurs.

While introverts may not be the first to take the microphone or dominate a room with their presence, their deep thinking, focused work, and high empathy are assets that enable them to build sustainable, innovative businesses. In this chapter, we'll explore the introvert advantage—the set of strengths that introverts bring to entrepreneurship—and why quiet power can often outperform loud charisma.

From solitude to focus and empathy, introverts are often more equipped than they realize to thrive in business. Their journey may look different from the traditional extroverted path, but their way is equally valuable and necessary in today's business world. The time has come for introverts to step into their unique power and recognize that introversion is not a barrier to success, but rather a competitive advantage.

1. Traits That Make Introverts Exceptional Entrepreneurs

The Power of Deep Thinking and Reflection

One of the greatest strengths of introverts is their ability to think deeply and reflect on situations, problems, and decisions. In a world that often values quick decision-making and fast action, introverts tend to take a more thoughtful and deliberate approach. This ability to reflect and analyze situations thoroughly allows introverted entrepreneurs to make informed, well-considered choices. They don't rush into decisions but instead take the time to assess risks and benefits, leading to better long-term outcomes for their businesses.

Real-life example:

- **Elon Musk,** widely known for his groundbreaking work with companies like Tesla and SpaceX, is often categorized as an introvert. Musk has admitted to spending long hours alone, focusing on intricate details, and using his deep thinking to innovate in industries that others thought were impossible to change. His ability to think critically and reflect deeply has been key to his success.

Focused Work: Embracing the Power of Solitude

Introverts tend to work best in quiet, uninterrupted environments, where they can focus intensely on their tasks. This ability to concentrate deeply, without the distraction of constant social interaction or noise, gives introverts a distinct advantage when it comes to problem-solving, innovation, and productivity.

While extroverts may thrive in high-energy, social environments, introverts often find their most productive and creative moments in solitude. This makes them particularly skilled at tackling complex challenges, researching new ideas, and working through problems that require focus and concentration.

Real-life example:

- **Bill Gates**, the co-founder of Microsoft, is another well-known introvert who credits much of his success to his ability to work deeply and with focus. Gates has often spoken about his love for time alone, where he could focus on reading, learning, and thinking about how to solve the world's toughest problems. His business success has been built on his ability to think deeply, something introverts excel at.

Creativity and Innovation in Solitude

Introverts are often more creative than they give themselves credit for. The space and solitude they enjoy foster a creative process that leads to new ideas, innovative solutions, and fresh perspectives. Introverts may spend significant time reflecting on their ideas, which results in unique business models, products, or services.

For introverted entrepreneurs, creating the right environment to think deeply and reflect can lead to breakthroughs that drive their businesses forward. This creative energy, paired with their natural inclination to research and plan, allows introverts to develop innovative business strategies and solutions that can be market-leading.

Real-life example:

- Steve Wozniak, co-founder of Apple, is a perfect example of an introvert who created a revolutionary product through his ability to focus on detailed work and innovation. Wozniak spent countless hours alone in his garage working on the early prototypes of the Apple computer, far from the limelight but deeply immersed in the process of invention.

2. High Empathy and Emotional Intelligence

The Introvert's Superpower: Empathy

One of the defining traits of introverts is their high empathy—the ability to connect deeply with others' emotions, understand their needs, and respond in a way that fosters trust and collaboration. Introverts often prefer one-on-one interactions or small, intimate groups over large social gatherings, which gives them an edge when it comes to building strong, meaningful relationships in business.

Introverts' empathy allows them to connect with customers, employees, and business partners on a deeper level. By listening actively and understanding the emotions of others, introverts are able to build loyalty, trust, and rapport—which are key to any successful business. Whether it's understanding a customer's pain point or providing emotional support to an employee, introverts are well-suited to lead with compassion and understanding.

Real-life example:

- **Howard Schultz**, the former CEO of Starbucks, has been credited with creating a company culture that values empathy and emotional intelligence. Schultz, known for his introverted tendencies, built Starbucks by focusing on creating a welcoming environment for both employees and customers. His ability to understand the needs of others and build strong emotional connections was key to Starbucks' global success.

Building Strong, Trust-Based Relationships

Because introverts tend to listen more than speak, they are often able to build trust and rapport more quickly than their extroverted counterparts. They focus on understanding the perspectives of others and tend to act with integrity, which establishes strong business relationships.

In leadership roles, introverts often take a more servant-leader approach, focusing on helping their employees grow and supporting their needs. They excel in creating workplaces where individuals feel valued and supported, leading to higher engagement, greater job satisfaction, and improved performance.

Real-life example:

- **Tim Cook**, the current CEO of Apple, is often cited as an introvert who has led with empathy and humility. Cook is known for his listening skills and his ability to understand the emotions and needs of those around him. His approach to leadership has allowed him to build a loyal and highly engaged team at Apple.

3. Comparing Quiet Power with Loud Charisma

The Loud Charisma Trap

In many traditional business settings, there's an overemphasis on charisma—the ability to charm, persuade, and influence others through boldness and strong presence. While these traits can be beneficial, they often obscure the importance of quiet power. Loud, extroverted leaders often dominate conversations, and their influence can sometimes be based on personality rather than substance.

Introverts, however, have a quiet power that stems from their ability to lead with thoughtfulness, deliberation, and empathy. Instead of trying to impress others with bold statements, introverts focus on listening carefully, thinking critically, and making decisions based on solid reasoning. Their ability to lead with a calm demeanor often earns them respect and loyalty, rather than superficial admiration.

The Quiet Leader's Impact

While extroverts may be great at selling ideas quickly or getting people excited with their charisma, introverts excel at sustained influence—building trust over time, delivering results consistently, and leading with humility. Introverts do not need to dominate the conversation or stand at the front to make an impact. Their quiet leadership style allows them to inspire long-term commitment and cultivate an environment where people feel valued and respected.

The quiet leader's impact is often less about flashy presentations and more about substantive results and the lasting relationships they create. Their leadership may be subtle, but it's often far-reaching.

Quiet Leadership and the Modern Business World

The business world is gradually recognizing that extroversion is not the only path to leadership success. Quiet leadership is not only possible, but it's also becoming a powerful and necessary approach in today's rapidly changing world. As more businesses prioritize emotional intelligence, diversity, and sustainable growth, introverted leaders are proving that quieter, thoughtful leadership styles are more than adequate—they are ideal for navigating the complexities of modern business.

Conclusion: Harnessing the Introvert Advantage

Introverts may not always get the same attention or recognition as their extroverted counterparts, but they bring essential qualities to the table that make them not only effective leaders but exceptional entrepreneurs. Deep thinking, focused work, and empathy allow introverts to succeed in ways that go beyond loud charisma and quick decision-making.

By leveraging these inherent strengths, introverts can build businesses that are resilient, innovative, and impactful. Quiet power isn't about withdrawing or being passive—it's about leading with thoughtful intention, emotional intelligence, and long-term vision. Introverted entrepreneurs don't need to fit into the mold of the loud, charismatic leader. They can carve out their own path, embracing their quiet strengths and becoming powerful, respected leaders in their own right.

This chapter serves as a reminder that true leadership comes from within and that introverts have a unique advantage in today's business world. By embracing your introverted qualities, you can build a business that reflects your values, vision, and capacity for sustained impact. The quiet climb to success may take time, but it is a climb that, when done with intention, can result in unshakable business success.

Chapter 3
Building Confidence Without Performing

Introduction: The Quiet Confidence of Authentic Leadership

Confidence in business is often mistaken for performance—the ability to be outgoing, assertive, and publicly engaging. The modern world tends to equate confidence with visibility, with the loudest voice or the most charismatic personality leading the way. This is particularly true in the corporate environment where extroversion is often seen as the primary route to success. However, for introverts, this idea can be alienating and draining. The truth is that confidence does not have to be loud or performance-based; it can stem from internal validation, authenticity, and the ability to remain true to oneself without the need to fit into society's expectations of what a leader should look like.

In this chapter, we will explore how to build confidence from within, avoiding the trap of seeking external validation or performing in ways that feel unnatural. By embracing quiet confidence, introverts can become powerful leaders, entrepreneurs, and collaborators without feeling the need to fake extroversion. We'll also discuss how to manage social exhaustion, a common challenge for introverts, and provide practical strategies to ensure that you can show up authentically without draining your energy.

Building true confidence is about accepting yourself for who you are, not who the world expects you to be. Grounding routines and daily rituals will help introverts stay connected to their inner strengths and reduce social burnout. By the end of this chapter, you will have a deeper understanding of how to cultivate a sense of confidence that is rooted in authenticity, reflection, and self-empowerment.

1. Developing Internal Validation Over External Applause

The Need for External Validation in a Performance-Driven World

The world often reinforces the idea that success and confidence come from external validation. Whether it's through praise from bosses, accolades from peers, or the affirmation of social media followers, external recognition is often perceived as the benchmark for achievement. However, this outward pursuit of approval can be draining, particularly for introverts, who may not naturally seek the spotlight or thrive in environments that require constant affirmation.

The problem with relying on external validation is that it places the power of your self-worth in the hands of others. This can lead to a cycle of seeking constant approval, and can cause insecurity when that validation is not forthcoming. Introverts, who might naturally shy away from seeking praise, often feel disconnected from this performance-based success. But the key to sustainable confidence lies in the ability to develop internal validation—the practice of accepting and affirming your own worth, regardless of external circumstances.

What is Internal Validation?

Internal validation is the process of recognizing your own worth and embracing your strengths without needing approval from others. It involves self-acceptance and self-reflection, building confidence through self-assurance rather than seeking constant reassurance from external sources. When you rely on internal validation, you begin to view success as something that is defined by your own standards, values, and goals, rather than the external opinions or expectations of others.

Internal validation helps create a solid foundation of self-esteem. When you can affirm your own worth and accomplishments, you no longer need external praise to feel accomplished. Your self-worth is not tied to how others perceive you, but instead, how you view yourself. This shift allows you to stay authentic, remain focused on your own goals, and achieve success on your own terms.

Real-life example:

- **Sophia,** a 45-year-old entrepreneur, had spent much of her career seeking validation from her peers and superiors. Her desire for external approval led her to take on projects that didn't align with her true passions, simply to gain recognition. After a period of burnout, Sophia began focusing on her internal validation. She created a daily reflection routine, where she listed her achievements and affirmed her abilities. Over time, Sophia's confidence grew—not because of external recognition, but because she had come to accept and value herself for the work she was doing. This shift allowed her to run a business that felt authentic, aligned with her values, and fulfilling.

2. How to Show Up Authentically Without Faking Extroversion

The Pressure to Perform

Society often values extroverted traits such as boldness, outspoken opinions, and public speaking, introverts can feel like they need to perform in order to succeed. This can be particularly challenging in environments where extroversion is rewarded—from sales teams to corporate leadership roles, there is often a presumption that success requires being charismatic, outgoing, and visible. This assumption can leave introverts feeling as though they have to fake extroversion in order to gain recognition and succeed.

However, the truth is that authenticity is far more powerful than any performance. When introverts try to mimic extroverted behaviors, they often feel drained and inauthentic, leading to burnout and frustration. The key to success for introverts lies in learning how to show up authentically while still making an impact in business, leadership, and personal endeavors.

Embrace Your Unique Strengths

Instead of forcing yourself to fit the traditional extroverted mold, embrace the qualities that make you a strong, quiet leader. Introverts possess qualities like deep listening, strategic thinking, patience, and empathy—traits that are just as important in business as being able to sell loudly or lead a meeting. Recognize that your quiet presence can still command respect, foster collaboration, and create an environment of trust and authenticity.

The key is to show up authentically in the spaces you occupy, without pretending to be someone you are not. Whether it's in team meetings, client presentations, or public speaking events, introverts can excel by tapping into their unique strengths and leading with authenticity. Focus on what you bring to the table—whether it's your ability to listen deeply, analyze complex problems, or lead with empathy—and let those strengths shine.

Real-life example:

- **Mike**, an introverted CEO of a small tech company, faced the challenge of leading his team in a way that felt true to his nature. Initially, he tried to adopt more extroverted behaviors, speaking up in meetings more frequently and trying to network at industry events. However, he quickly felt drained and disconnected. Instead of continuing to fake extroversion, Mike embraced his natural style of quiet leadership—leading by example, listening attentively to his team, and providing thoughtful feedback. His team responded positively, as they felt heard and supported, and Mike's business thrived without the need for loud performances.

Embrace Quiet Leadership

Being an introvert doesn't mean you cannot lead effectively. In fact, quiet leaders often excel in environments where thoughtful reflection, deep thinking, and emotional intelligence are valued. Quiet leaders are able to inspire loyalty, trust, and respect because they don't rely on charisma or loud displays of power; instead, they lead with integrity, vision, and humility. They understand that leadership is not about taking the spotlight, but about empowering others and creating an environment where everyone can succeed.

Real-life example:

- **Bill Gates**, the co-founder of Microsoft, is a prime example of a quiet, introverted leader who has reshaped industries. Gates is known for his reserved nature and strategic thinking. While many might expect a CEO to be a loud, extroverted figure, Gates has demonstrated that quiet leadership can lead to profound success. His leadership style—focused on listening, learning, and strategic decision-making—has been instrumental in Microsoft's growth and impact on the tech industry.

3. Grounding Routines and Rituals to Reduce Social Exhaustion

Social Exhaustion: Understanding the Toll on Introverts

For introverts, constant social interaction can be mentally and physically draining. Unlike extroverts who gain energy from socializing, introverts typically find that engaging with others for extended periods leaves them feeling exhausted and overwhelmed. In business, this social fatigue can manifest in stress, burnout, and a diminished ability to focus. It's essential for introverts to recognize the importance of balance and self-care in maintaining their mental and emotional well-being.

Introverts need time for solitude and quiet reflection to recharge. Without this downtime, introverts may find themselves unable to perform at their best, both in personal and professional settings. The key to maintaining a sustainable business and leadership path is learning how to manage social fatigue effectively.

Establishing Grounding Rituals

Introverts can mitigate the effects of social exhaustion by developing grounding routines that help them regain energy and maintain a sense of balance. Grounding rituals are simple, intentional practices that bring you back to yourself—allowing you to reset, recharge, and refocus. Some examples of grounding rituals include:

1. **Morning meditation or mindfulness practices**: Begin your day with a few moments of reflection to center your mind and body.

2. **Scheduled solo time**: Carve out periods of your day where you can engage in solo activities, such as reading, writing, or taking a walk, to recharge.

3. **Breathing exercises**: Practice deep breathing or **progressive muscle relaxation** to reduce stress and clear your mind.

4. **Creative outlets**: Engage in a hobby or creative activity that allows you to express yourself without the pressure of external validation.

By incorporating grounding rituals into your routine, you can ensure that you stay connected to your authentic self and avoid the burnout that often comes from social exhaustion.

Real-life example:

- **Sarah**, a 50-year-old marketing consultant, found that she became exhausted after long client meetings and networking events. To manage her energy, Sarah implemented a grounding ritual of daily journaling and morning walks. These practices allowed her to decompress, reflect on her day, and reset before diving into her next business task. Over time, Sarah found that she could engage more effectively in meetings and maintain her energy throughout the day by integrating these rituals into her routine.

Conclusion: Quiet Confidence, Bold Leadership

Building confidence without performing is about embracing who you are—quiet strengths and all. Introverts have an incredible capacity for leadership, entrepreneurship, and creativity, but their power lies in their authenticity, thoughtful approach, and empathy. By developing internal validation, showing up authentically, and incorporating grounding routines into your daily life, introverts can build a strong sense of confidence that is rooted in who they truly are.

Confidence doesn't need to be loud. It doesn't need to be flashy or performative. True confidence comes from within, and it's this quiet strength that often leads to the most meaningful and lasting success. For introverts, the journey to success is not about changing who you are, but about embracing your unique qualities and letting them shine. Quiet confidence is the foundation for strong leadership, sustainable success, and a fulfilling life.

PART II
DESIGNING A BUSINESS THAT FITS YOU

Chapter 4

Quiet Branding – Attract Without the Hype

Introduction: The Power of Quiet Branding

In the noisy, attention-driven world of business, where extroverted entrepreneurs dominate the conversation with charisma, flashy marketing, and loud promotions, introverts may feel sidelined or reluctant to take part. But as the business landscape evolves, it's becoming clearer that quiet branding—the ability to attract, engage, and build a loyal following without resorting to the typical loud, over-the-top tactics—is not only possible but also deeply effective.

This chapter is dedicated to helping introverts understand how they can build a personal brand that is both magnetic and authentic, without having to fake extroverted behaviors. We'll explore how to define your brand with clarity, rather than relying on charisma, how to tell your story in a way that feels subtle yet compelling, and how to create content that reflects your natural energy. Introverts can build powerful brands by focusing on authenticity, empathy, and strategic thinking, allowing them to create meaningful connections with their audience while staying true to themselves.

Building a quiet brand is about focusing on quality, authenticity, and consistency. It's not about shouting to be heard; it's about crafting an experience that resonates with the right people, one that aligns with your values, vision, and strengths. Quiet branding is strategic, deliberate, and deeply personal—and it can be just as successful as any "louder" approach in attracting and retaining customers.

1. Personal Branding for Introverts: Clarity Over Charisma

The Challenge of Traditional Branding

In many business circles, personal branding is often equated with charisma—the ability to charm others with your presence, wit, and energy. Extroverted entrepreneurs have long been lauded for their ability to dominate a room, speak confidently, and project an image that seems larger than life. However, introverts often feel uncomfortable with these assumptions, as their natural style is far more subtle, reflective, and quiet. So, how can introverts compete in a world where branding often feels like a performance?

The answer lies in shifting the focus from charisma to clarity. While extroverted entrepreneurs rely on their ability to attract attention with energy and enthusiasm, introverts can focus on articulating their value clearly, highlighting their expertise, and creating a brand that speaks for itself through authenticity and integrity.

For introverts, personal branding isn't about being the loudest or the most visible; it's about finding clarity in your message and purpose. It's about communicating who you are, what you offer, and why your business matters in a way that is consistent and true to your values. This is quiet branding at its core: it's about purposeful messaging that doesn't rely on theatrics but instead on a strong, consistent presence that speaks volumes in its own quiet way.

Defining Your Brand with Purpose

The foundation of any strong personal brand is a clear understanding of your values, mission, and vision. Introverts excel at introspection and deep thinking, which makes them uniquely positioned to define their brand with clarity and purpose. By starting with a solid personal mission, introverts can build a brand that resonates with authenticity.

To begin the process of defining your personal brand, ask yourself the following questions:

- **What are my core values?** What do I stand for, and how can I integrate these values into my business?

- **What unique perspective or expertise do I offer?** What makes me different from others in my field?

- **How do I want people to feel when they interact with my brand?** Do I want to inspire trust, creativity, innovation, or compassion?

- **What is the long-term vision for my business?** How do I want my brand to evolve over time?

Once you've answered these questions, you'll have a clearer sense of how to shape your brand messaging in a way that's authentic, consistent, and focused. Introverts have the advantage of being able to articulate their values and vision in a way that is deeply thoughtful, and this reflective approach to branding often leads to a more meaningful and purpose-driven brand.

2. How to Tell Your Story in a Subtle, Magnetic Way

The Power of Storytelling for Introverts

Storytelling is one of the most powerful tools for building a personal brand, and introverts are naturally adept at weaving narratives that are both compelling and relatable. While extroverts may rely on grand gestures or dramatic presentations, introverts tend to excel in more subtle, nuanced storytelling—an approach that often resonates more deeply with audiences.

Telling your story is about sharing your journey, your challenges, and your victories in a way that is both authentic and approachable. Introverts have the unique ability to create intimate connections with their audience, drawing them in with their vulnerability, insight, and thoughtfulness. The key to magnetic storytelling is to speak from the heart and allow your authentic self to shine through.

Real-life example:

- **Maya Angelou**, one of the most beloved authors of the 20th century, is a perfect example of a quiet, magnetic storyteller. While she was an introvert, her words carried immense power. Angelou's ability to express profound truths in a way that was deeply personal and reflective made her work resonate with millions of people worldwide. She didn't rely on performance; she simply shared her authentic experiences with the world.

Crafting Your Narrative

To build a compelling personal brand, start by thinking about the story you want to tell. This could be the story of how you started your business, the challenges you've faced, or the values that have driven your decisions. Here are a few steps to help you create your narrative:

- **Start with authenticity**: Don't try to fit into a mold of what you think a leader or entrepreneur should be. Share your story honestly, including the struggles and setbacks you've faced. People connect with stories that are real and relatable.

- **Focus on your "why"**: Why did you start your business? What drives you to keep going? Share the deeper motivations behind your work and how it aligns with your values. This will help your audience understand your purpose and connect with your mission.

- **Use vulnerability as strength**: Don't shy away from sharing moments of vulnerability. Introverts often excel at connecting with others on a deeper level, and sharing your own challenges or insecurities can make you more relatable and trusted.

- **Keep it concise and focused**: While storytelling is important, introverts excel at being succinct. Instead of telling long-winded stories, focus on the key moments that define your journey and illustrate your values.

Real-life example:

- **Oprah Winfrey**, one of the most influential women in media, is a master at authentic storytelling. Oprah's rise to success was not through loud performances but through the power of vulnerability and sharing her personal experiences with her audience. Her ability to tell stories that resonate on an emotional level has made her a household name.

3. Creating Content That Reflects Your Energy

The Difference Between "Loud" Content and "Quiet" Content

In a world where content is often expected to be loud, attention-grabbing, and full of hype, introverts have an advantage in creating content that is authentic, thoughtful, and aligned with their natural energy. While extroverted content creators may focus on high-energy videos or viral campaigns, introverts can create content that resonates with their audience on a deeper level.

Quiet content is about creating material that reflects your unique voice and energy, whether that's through written posts, podcasts, videos, or other forms of media. Introverts often do best with content that doesn't require constant performance or social interaction. Instead, they can focus on creating value through reflection, insight, and authenticity.

How to Create Content That Feels Authentic

- **Find your voice**: Your content should reflect who you are. If you are naturally reserved, then let your content reflect that. If you are thoughtful and introspective, use your platform to share deep insights or personal reflections that align with your core beliefs. Authenticity is magnetic, and your audience will appreciate your honesty and vulnerability.

- **Use long-form content**: Introverts often excel in long-form content, such as blog posts, articles, or eBooks, where they can express their ideas more fully. This type of content allows you to delve deeper into your thoughts, ideas, and values without having to perform or condense your message.

- **Create with purpose**: When creating content, always ask yourself: What do I want my audience to walk away with? Introverts are strategic and thoughtful, so use this to your advantage by creating content that provides real value to your audience, whether through educational material, personal stories, or thoughtful analysis.

Real-life example:

- **Cal Newport**, author of "Deep Work", is a perfect example of someone who has built a quiet brand with content that speaks to introverts and individuals seeking to escape the noise of the modern world. Newport's work is deeply thoughtful, reflective, and provides tangible value to readers without flashy marketing tactics or loud performances.

Conclusion: Quiet Branding as a Powerful Strategy

Quiet branding is not about shrinking into the background or hiding your strengths. It's about embracing your natural introverted tendencies to create a powerful, authentic brand that resonates with your audience on a deep level. Introverts do not need to perform or fake extroversion in order to build a meaningful, influential business. Instead, they can focus on clarity, authenticity, and thoughtfulness—traits that form the bedrock of a successful brand.

By focusing on internal validation, authentic storytelling, and purpose-driven content, introverts can build brands that reflect their true selves and attract loyal customers. Quiet branding doesn't require shouting to be heard; it's about speaking with intention and building lasting relationships through value, insight, and authenticity. For introverts, the power of branding lies in their ability to stay true to who they are, create meaningful content, and lead with quiet confidence.

Chapter 5

Selling Without the Sleaze

Introduction: Redefining Sales with Integrity

In the fast-paced world of modern business, sales is often a noisy, high-pressure game dominated by aggressive tactics, pushy marketing, and the constant pursuit of conversions. For many introverts and those who prefer a more subtle approach, the typical sales process can feel uncomfortable, disingenuous, or even sleazy. "Selling" is often associated with flashy pitches, hard sales, and manipulative tactics—none of which feel authentic or aligned with the values of many entrepreneurs.

However, the truth is that sales doesn't have to be aggressive or sleazy. In fact, the best sales strategies are the ones that prioritize relationship-building, empathy, and authenticity. Whether you're an introvert, someone who dislikes the high-energy hustle, or just someone who wants to do business in a more ethical and sustainable way, there are gentle and effective sales strategies that can help you sell without the sleaze.

This chapter is dedicated to showing you how to sell in a way that feels authentic, values-driven, and respectful of your potential customers' needs. We'll explore gentle sales tactics that focus on building trust, listening deeply, and offering solutions that truly serve your audience. In addition, we will dive into email funnels, webinars, and soft-sell techniques—all tools that allow you to engage with customers in a non-pushy, non-intrusive way while still generating sales.

By the end of this chapter, you will have a deeper understanding of how to sell with integrity, create authentic relationships with your customers, and grow your business without resorting to traditional sales tactics that feel manipulative or uncomfortable.

1. Gentle Sales Strategies that Align with Your Values

The Shift Toward Authentic Sales

Sales have evolved over time. No longer does the hard-sell approach—where you're constantly pushing and convincing customers to buy—hold the same power. Instead, customers now look for genuine relationships, trustworthiness, and value in the brands they support. As a result, many entrepreneurs have adopted a more gentle, ethical approach to sales that puts the customer's needs first.

For introverts or those who are uncomfortable with aggressive sales tactics, this is a welcomed change. Gentle sales strategies are about creating an environment of mutual respect, where the focus is not solely on closing the deal but on offering solutions, building trust, and nurturing a long-term relationship.

Here are several elements of a gentle sales strategy that aligns with values-based selling:

- **Focus on building relationships**: The first step in selling without the sleaze is building a relationship with your potential customers. This doesn't mean trying to get them to buy immediately, but rather offering them value through your knowledge, expertise, and understanding of their pain points. Take the time to get to know your customer's needs and challenges, so you can offer them a solution that truly works for them.

- **Educate rather than push**: The goal of your sales approach should be to educate your audience, not force them into a sale. Offer valuable content, whether through blog posts, videos, or social media, that addresses your audience's questions, provides insights, and highlights your expertise. By giving people the information they need, you position yourself as a trusted advisor rather than a pushy salesperson.

- **Be transparent and authentic**: Authenticity is key when building trust with potential customers. Be honest about what you can offer and don't overpromise. If your product or service isn't the right fit for someone, don't hesitate to tell them. Transparency builds trust, and customers appreciate honesty. When you align your sales tactics with your values, you build long-term credibility and loyalty.

- **Create an emotional connection**: Sales aren't just about transactions; they are about relationships. When you engage with customers on an emotional level, you create a bond that goes beyond the product or service being sold. Understand the emotional motivations behind your customers' needs, and offer them something that truly resonates with their desires and aspirations.

Empathy-Driven Sales

At the core of gentle sales strategies is empathy. Empathy is the ability to understand and share the feelings of another person. It allows you to connect with your customers on a human level, and it helps you build trust and respect. Empathy is particularly important in today's sales environment, where customers are increasingly seeking brands that align with their values and genuinely care about their needs.

Empathy-driven sales go beyond just understanding a customer's problem; it's about actively listening and then offering a solution that's tailored to their unique situation. By putting yourself in the customer's shoes and focusing on their pain points, you are positioning yourself as a trusted advisor, not just a salesperson.

Real-life example:

- **Patagonia**, an outdoor clothing brand, is a great example of a company that uses empathy-driven sales strategies. The brand's focus on sustainability, environmental activism, and ethical production practices resonates deeply with its customers. Patagonia's sales approach is not about pushing products but rather about educating customers on the importance of environmental consciousness and offering them a chance to contribute to that cause. By connecting with their customers' values, Patagonia has built a loyal following that doesn't just buy products—they buy into the brand's mission.

2. Building Trust Through Listening and Thoughtful Offers

Listening as the Foundation of Trust

One of the most effective ways to sell without being pushy is to listen actively to your potential customers. By truly understanding their needs, pain points, and goals, you can position your offer as a solution that is tailored to them. Active listening helps you not only understand what the customer is asking for but also what they are not saying—their underlying concerns, fears, and aspirations.

Instead of jumping straight into a sales pitch, take the time to ask open-ended questions and allow the conversation to flow. By listening, you're showing the customer that you care about their unique situation, which builds trust and rapport. When a customer feels heard, they are much more likely to trust your recommendations and move forward with your offer.

Real-life example:

- **Simon Sinek**, an author and motivational speaker, often speaks about the importance of listening in leadership and sales. He emphasizes that when leaders and salespeople take the time to listen, they create trust and understanding. His approach is centered around understanding people's motivations and connecting with them on a deeper level, which leads to stronger relationships and more successful sales.

Crafting Thoughtful Offers

Once you've listened carefully to your customer's needs, it's time to offer them a thoughtful solution. A thoughtful offer is not just about pushing a product or service; it's about offering a solution that addresses their specific pain points and aligns with their goals. It's important to frame your offer in terms of how it benefits the customer, rather than focusing solely on the features of the product or service.

Be sure to customize your offer based on the conversation you've had with the customer. Introverts excel at understanding nuances, which gives them the ability to offer personalized solutions that feel more authentic and genuine. Tailor your messaging, highlight the value, and make it clear how your product or service will improve their lives or solve a specific problem.

3. Email Funnels, Webinars, and Soft-Sell Techniques

Email Funnels: Nurturing Relationships Without the Push

An email funnel is a sequence of emails that guide a potential customer through the sales journey. Unlike traditional hard-sell techniques, email funnels provide value-driven content that nurtures the relationship over time. Introverts can excel in this arena by creating meaningful and helpful content that addresses the needs of their audience while avoiding the pressure of immediate sales.

In an email funnel, you're not just selling a product; you're building trust and providing educational content that positions you as a thought leader. A well-crafted funnel offers valuable insights, tips, and guidance that help your audience make informed decisions at their own pace.

Real-life example:

- **Marie Forleo**, an entrepreneur and creator of B-School, has built a highly successful business using email marketing funnels. Instead of simply pushing products, Forleo uses her funnels to provide value-driven content that nurtures relationships and builds trust with her audience over time. Her funnel includes free webinars, email courses, and insightful blog posts, all designed to educate and empower her audience. By offering value first, Forleo creates a natural path to conversion that feels authentic and gentle.

Webinars: Providing Value Through Live Engagement

Webinars are an excellent way to engage with your audience in a more personalized, interactive, and non-salesy manner. By offering free webinars that provide real value to your audience, you can position yourself as an expert without pushing for an immediate sale. Webinars allow you to showcase your knowledge, answer questions, and provide solutions that align with your audience's needs.

The key to a successful webinar is to focus on value delivery rather than hard-selling. Use the webinar as an opportunity to build a relationship, answer questions, and provide actionable insights. At the end of the webinar, offer a soft-sell invitation to your product or service—one that feels like a natural extension of the content you've just shared.

Soft-Sell Techniques: Selling Through Subtlety

A soft-sell approach focuses on providing value to the customer and allowing them to make a decision on their own, rather than using high-pressure tactics. Introverts excel at soft-selling techniques because they allow them to build relationships and earn trust over time. Whether it's through email marketing, content creation, or live engagements, the goal is to create a natural path to conversion without feeling the need to be overly persuasive.

Some key elements of the soft-sell approach include:

- **Providing value upfront**: Whether through content, resources, or education, give your audience something they can use.

- **Building relationships**: Focus on long-term relationships rather than immediate transactions.

- **Highlighting benefits over features**: Frame your offer in terms of how it solves problems or improves lives.

Conclusion: Authentic Sales as a Path to Sustainable Success

Selling doesn't have to be loud, aggressive, or disingenuous. By embracing gentle sales strategies that prioritize relationship-building, empathy, and authenticity, introverts can build successful businesses without the need for sleazy tactics. Through active listening, thoughtful offers, and value-driven content, you can connect with customers in a way that feels both natural and meaningful.

Ultimately, the best sales are not about convincing others to buy something they don't need; they are about building trust, providing value, and offering solutions that align with the needs of your audience. By adopting a more subtle, values-driven approach to sales, you can grow your business in a way that feels aligned with your own values and creates lasting relationships with your customers. Selling without the sleaze is about selling with integrity—something that introverts can do incredibly well.

Chapter 6

Building Systems to Speak for You

Introduction: The Power of Behind-the-Scenes Systems for Introverts

As an introvert, the idea of constantly being "on," whether in meetings, on social media, or in sales interactions, can be both mentally and emotionally draining. For many introverts, the need for constant engagement and performance can feel overwhelming. However, the modern business landscape offers powerful tools and systems that can help you reduce the energy required for real-time interactions while still driving business growth and maintaining a strong presence. The solution lies in the use of automation, evergreen content, and efficient backend systems that do the heavy lifting for you.

In this chapter, we will explore how to build systems that allow you to scale your business effectively without constantly draining your personal energy. From automations that handle repetitive tasks, to evergreen content that continues to provide value long after it's been created, the goal is to create a business infrastructure that works for you, not the other way around. This chapter will also delve into how to create processes that allow your business to function smoothly and efficiently, freeing up time for you to focus on what truly matters—whether that's big-picture strategy, personal reflection, or pursuing your creative passions.

By implementing systems that speak for you and work autonomously, you can leverage your time, expertise, and resources to build a sustainable business that runs effectively in the background, all while maintaining your mental and emotional well-being. Let's dive into the tools and strategies that can help you create these systems and unlock your business's full potential.

1. Automations, Evergreen Content, and Systems That Reduce "Live" Energy Drains

The Necessity of Automating Repetitive Tasks

Entrepreneurs, especially introverts, often struggle with the energy drain that comes with constant, real-time interactions. Responding to emails, posting on social media, or dealing with customer service inquiries can quickly become overwhelming, leaving little time for strategic thinking or deep work. The key to solving this problem is automation— using tools that handle repetitive tasks, allowing you to conserve your mental energy while keeping your business running smoothly.

In business, automation can take many forms. From automated email marketing sequences to customer relationship management (CRM) systems, automations enable you to communicate with clients and deliver content without being constantly present. For example, you can set up automated email sequences to nurture leads, onboard new clients, and maintain ongoing communication without ever having to manually write each email.

One of the most effective ways to automate your business is by creating email funnels that guide potential customers through your sales process. With well-designed email automation, your system can respond to inquiries, nurture leads, and even convert customers without you needing to be actively involved. This helps reduce the need for constant engagement, giving you more time to focus on what matters most— whether that's building your products or refining your strategy.

Using Evergreen Content for Long-Term Impact

Evergreen content refers to material that remains relevant and valuable to your audience over time. Unlike content that has a limited shelf life, such as time-sensitive news articles or trend-based posts, evergreen content provides ongoing value and continues to attract and engage customers long after it's published. For introverts, evergreen content is a game-changer because it allows you to produce high-quality material once and watch it generate leads and traffic without requiring continual effort.

Examples of evergreen content include:

- **Blog posts** that address common pain points and questions in your industry.

- **Webinars** that provide valuable insights and can be automated for ongoing viewing.

- **How-to guides** and tutorials that remain relevant to new customers at any time.

- **Email courses** that can be set up to auto-enroll participants over time.

Introverts excel at creating content that is reflective, detailed, and useful. By leveraging evergreen content, you can create a content library that continues to drive traffic and leads while minimizing the need for continuous real-time involvement. This allows you to reach more people without the pressure of constantly being "on" or engaging in one-on-one interactions.

Real-life example:

- **Pat Flynn,** the founder of Smart Passive Income, is a prime example of an entrepreneur who has built a thriving business by leveraging evergreen content. Through his podcast, blog posts, and online courses, Pat generates passive income through content that continues to attract new listeners and students over time. His approach allows him to maintain a steady income without constantly engaging in live interactions, which aligns with his introverted nature.

Customer Service Automations and CRM Tools

For introverts, customer service can often be a major source of energy drain. Answering questions, responding to complaints, and managing customer expectations can feel like an endless cycle of communication. However, by integrating customer relationship management (CRM) tools into your business, you can streamline communication and reduce the emotional labor required for client interactions.

CRM systems allow you to automate responses to frequently asked questions, send follow-up emails, and track customer interactions in one place. Additionally, you can use chatbots or automated help desks to answer common inquiries, ensuring that your customers receive the support they need without requiring your constant involvement.

2. Creating Processes That Scale Quietly

The Importance of Process Building

To build a business that operates smoothly and sustainably, you need to create processes that are scalable and efficient. These systems and workflows ensure that your business can continue to grow without requiring increased input from you at every step. The beauty of having well-defined processes is that they allow you to delegate tasks, automate workflows, and free up time for more strategic endeavors.

Here are a few key areas where introverts can benefit from creating scalable processes:

- **Content creation**: Instead of constantly coming up with new content ideas or formats, create a process that allows you to repurpose content for different platforms. For example, you can turn blog posts into social media posts, podcasts, or videos with minimal extra effort. By creating content once and using it in multiple ways, you maximize your impact while minimizing the energy spent on creation.

- **Lead generation**: Set up processes that capture leads efficiently and automatically, such as opt-in forms, landing pages, and webinar funnels. Once leads are captured, you can nurture them through automated email sequences or add them to a CRM system that keeps track of their progress.

- **Client onboarding**: Simplify and standardize your onboarding process so that you can efficiently manage new clients without needing to be involved in every step. This could include automated emails, welcome packets, or resources that get sent out to new clients as soon as they sign up.

Creating scalable processes doesn't mean losing personal touch; it means streamlining your operations to make your work more efficient and sustainable in the long run. The systems you build should allow your business to grow without requiring constant hands-on involvement.

Building a Team That Runs the Systems

Introverts thrive in environments where they can focus on strategy, content creation, and problem-solving. Once you've created systems that are scalable, consider building a remote team or leveraging freelancers to help execute the systems you've put in place. This allows you to stay involved in the aspects of your business that you enjoy and excel at, while others manage the day-to-day operations.

For example, you might bring on a virtual assistant to manage your email funnels, or hire a social media manager to schedule posts and engage with your community online. With the right team in place, you can ensure that your systems are executed efficiently without needing to be involved in every detail.

3. Letting Your Backend Do the Heavy Lifting

Streamlining Your Backend for Efficiency

The backend of your business is where all the operational systems and tools live. For introverts, this is a critical area because it allows you to focus on the creative, strategic, and innovative parts of your business, while the backend systems handle the more administrative tasks. By setting up an efficient backend, you ensure that your business continues to run smoothly without requiring constant oversight from you.

Some areas of your backend to optimize for efficiency include:

- **Automated invoicing and payments**: Set up automated invoicing systems that send out bills, process payments, and track outstanding invoices without you needing to be involved.

- **Inventory and order management**: Use tools that track your products, sales, and customer orders automatically, so you can spend more time on strategy and less time managing day-to-day logistics.

- **Marketing automation**: Tools like Mailchimp, HubSpot, or ConvertKit allow you to automate your marketing campaigns, from sending newsletters to managing your customer journeys, so you don't have to manually handle each step.

Integrating Tools for Maximum Impact

To ensure your business runs efficiently, it's important to integrate the tools you use. This creates a seamless experience where your systems talk to each other, reducing the need for you to manage multiple platforms. For example, you can integrate your CRM with your email marketing system, so that once a lead is added to your database, they automatically enter your sales funnel without you needing to do anything.

Conclusion: The Quiet Power of Systematic Success

Introverts are often most successful when they are able to quietly and strategically manage their business operations. By focusing on systems that reduce the need for constant live interactions and engagement, introverts can create businesses that scale efficiently without draining their energy.

Through automated processes, evergreen content, and an effective backend infrastructure, introverts can continue to grow their businesses while preserving their mental energy, creativity, and authenticity. The key to building a successful business lies not in being constantly "on" but in designing a system that works for you—one that aligns with your natural strengths and allows you to focus on the bigger picture.

By letting your systems speak for you, you create a business that is sustainable, efficient, and aligned with your values. As you build these systems, remember that the power of quiet leadership and strategic thinking can have a profound impact on your business's success.

PART III
LEADING WITHOUT SHOUTING

Chapter 7

Silent Leadership in Action

Introduction: The Strength of Silent Leadership

In a world where leadership is often associated with loud speeches, high energy, and assertive action, it can be challenging for introverted leaders to find their place. Conventional business wisdom often lauds the extroverted "charismatic" leader who thrives on social interactions, visible authority, and commanding a room. However, the truth is that leadership is not always about being the loudest in the room; it's about influence, vision, and the ability to guide others toward success.

This chapter focuses on the power of silent leadership, an approach where presence, consistency, and calm authority are the cornerstones. Introverts, who may not feel comfortable in the spotlight, can leverage their natural strengths—such as deep listening, thoughtfulness, and self-awareness—to lead effectively. Silent leadership doesn't mean being passive or disengaged; rather, it's about guiding with integrity, empathy, and thoughtful decision-making. In fact, the quiet leader often creates stronger relationships, greater trust, and more sustainable results than those who lead through louder means.

By redefining leadership in this way, introverts can take pride in their ability to lead from within, with calm, consistency, and the unwavering ability to provide guidance when needed. In this chapter, we will explore how introverts can redefine leadership through their presence, how they can create psychological safety for their teams, and how they can make decisions with calm authority that inspires confidence and trust. Through these principles, introverts can build leadership styles that are just as powerful, if not more, than those associated with traditional extroverted leadership.

1. Redefining Leadership Through Presence and Consistency

The Power of Presence in Leadership

In the business world, there is often an expectation that leaders must speak loudly, be visible at all times, and constantly display their presence in meetings, networking events, and public settings. This expectation often leads to the misconception that introverts—who prefer solitude, quiet reflection, and less overt social interaction—cannot effectively lead.

However, silent leadership is not about absence; it's about creating a strong, steady presence that inspires confidence and trust. Introverted leaders are often highly attuned to their environment and can lead effectively through actions rather than words. They demonstrate their leadership qualities not through loud speeches or dramatic gestures but through their consistent actions, thoughtful decisions, and calm demeanor.

A key component of silent leadership is the ability to remain grounded and present in any situation, especially during moments of crisis or uncertainty. This consistent presence provides stability for teams and reassures them that their leader is someone they can rely on, even in challenging times.

The power of presence in leadership is about creating an environment where people feel safe, understood, and confident in their leader's ability to navigate complex situations. Introverts, who are typically calm and strategic, have a natural ability to lead with presence by being attentive listeners, thoughtful problem-solvers, and steady decision-makers.

Real-life example:

- **Warren Buffet**, often regarded as one of the world's most successful investors, is a prime example of silent leadership. Known for his introverted personality and preference for reflection, Buffet's leadership is rooted in his ability to listen, observe, and make decisions with quiet confidence. Rather than dominating the conversation, he lets his actions and insights speak for themselves, earning the respect and trust of his followers. His leadership style demonstrates how silence and consistency can foster strong leadership without the need for constant outward displays of power.

Consistency as a Pillar of Silent Leadership

The second key component of silent leadership is consistency. While many leaders thrive on the adrenaline rush of the spotlight, introverted leaders often operate in a more steady and measured manner. They lead with a clear sense of purpose, and their actions consistently reflect their values and vision. This consistency is what ultimately builds trust and respect among teams and collaborators.

Being consistent in leadership doesn't necessarily mean maintaining a rigid approach; rather, it involves being reliable and predictable in how you make decisions, interact with your team, and respond to challenges. Consistency provides stability in environments that may feel uncertain, giving others the confidence that their leader will always approach issues with calmness, consideration, and integrity.

Real-life example:

- **Jeff Bezos**, the founder of Amazon, is known for his consistent approach to business leadership. Despite the immense scale and pressure of his company, Bezos is known for making decisions based on long-term vision and sticking to core principles that have guided Amazon's growth. His consistency in leadership— emphasizing customer satisfaction, efficiency, and innovation— has shaped Amazon into one of the most powerful companies in the world. Bezos' ability to maintain a steady, consistent course, even through challenges, is a hallmark of quiet, powerful leadership.

2. Creating Psychological Safety for Your Team or Collaborators

What is Psychological Safety?

One of the most significant responsibilities of any leader, especially an introverted one, is to create psychological safety within their team or organization. Psychological safety is the belief that one will not be penalized or humiliated for speaking up, making mistakes, or offering new ideas. It's the assurance that all voices, regardless of rank or background, are respected and heard.

In high-performing teams, psychological safety is a critical ingredient for success. It encourages innovation, creativity, and collaboration, as team members feel comfortable expressing their thoughts and ideas without the fear of judgment or rejection. For introverts, creating psychological safety is one of the most powerful ways to lead without the need for constant visibility or loud directives.

How Introverts Create Psychological Safety

Introverted leaders excel at creating environments where their team members feel comfortable and valued. They do so by focusing on active listening, thoughtful feedback, and humility. Rather than dominating conversations or making snap decisions, introverts tend to approach team interactions with calm and consideration, which fosters a sense of security and trust.

Introverts create psychological safety by:

- **Being present**: Introverts tend to listen deeply and attentively, making others feel heard and understood. When a leader takes the time to listen carefully to team members' concerns and ideas, it creates an environment where people feel comfortable contributing without fear of dismissal.

- **Encouraging feedback**: Introverts often have a natural tendency to reflect before speaking, which allows them to offer thoughtful feedback that encourages growth rather than criticism. This type of feedback helps team members feel supported and empowered to improve their work.

- **Building trust**: By consistently showing up with humility, reliability, and respect, introverted leaders can build trust with their teams. When team members feel that their leader is approachable and consistent, they are more likely to open up and share their thoughts freely.

- **Respecting individual strengths**: Introverted leaders recognize the value in their team's diverse strengths and give their team members the space to shine in ways that feel comfortable to them. By creating an environment where people are not forced to act outside their comfort zones, introverts can help their team members feel safe and supported in their roles.

Real-life example:

- **Indra Nooyi**, the former CEO of PepsiCo, is often described as a leader who creates a psychologically safe environment for her team. Nooyi, known for her introverted nature, fostered an atmosphere of open communication and collaboration within PepsiCo, where employees felt empowered to express their opinions and contribute ideas. Her approach to leadership, which focused on empathy and listening to employees, helped her lead the company to remarkable success.

3. Making Decisions with Calm Authority

The Calm Authority of Quiet Leaders

One of the hallmarks of silent leadership is the ability to make decisions with calm authority. Introverted leaders often take a deliberative approach to decision-making. Instead of rushing to conclusions or relying on gut instinct, they carefully assess the situation, weigh their options, and consider the long-term implications of their choices. This level-headedness allows them to make sound decisions that inspire confidence and trust.

Introverts do not need to shout their authority to command respect. Their quiet authority is rooted in their ability to stay calm under pressure, think critically, and approach challenges with a level-headed, thoughtful demeanor. By leading with calmness and reason, introverts help their teams navigate complex situations with clarity and purpose.

How to Make Decisions with Calm Authority

To make decisions with calm authority, introverts should:

- **Trust their instincts**: While introverts may take longer to make decisions, they often have a strong intuition about the right course of action. Trusting your inner wisdom and having confidence in your ability to make thoughtful decisions is crucial for introverted leaders.

- **Consider the long-term impact**: Introverts tend to think strategically and are more likely to consider the long-term consequences of their decisions. By focusing on the bigger picture, introverts ensure that their decisions align with their values, vision, and mission.

- **Remain composed under pressure**: In times of crisis, introverts excel at remaining calm and collected, which allows them to make clear-headed decisions even in high-pressure situations. This sense of calm provides reassurance to their team and fosters trust in their leadership.

- **Seek input and collaborate**: Although introverts may prefer to work alone, they understand the value of seeking input from others. Making decisions collaboratively, while still maintaining ultimate responsibility, allows introverts to make well-informed choices that take multiple perspectives into account.

Real-life example:

- **Angela Merkel**, the former Chancellor of Germany, exemplified calm authority throughout her tenure. Known for her introverted nature, Merkel was praised for her measured decision-making, particularly during crises such as the European debt crisis and the refugee crisis. Her ability to remain composed, think critically, and lead with empathy made her one of the most respected leaders in the world.

Conclusion: Leading with Quiet Strength

Silent leadership is not about avoiding responsibility or shrinking away from tough decisions. It's about leading with integrity, empathy, and consistency. Introverts, with their deep thinking, strategic mindset, and natural ability to listen, have the unique ability to create a leadership style that is both calm and powerful.

By focusing on building trust, creating psychological safety, and making decisions with quiet authority, introverts can lead businesses, teams, and projects in a way that is sustainable, effective, and deeply impactful. In the world of business, leadership is not about how loud you can be; it's about how genuine and effective your actions are. Introverts, through silent leadership, have the ability to build teams that trust them, respect them, and follow them not because they dominate the room, but because they lead with thoughtfulness, humility, and vision.

Chapter 8

Managing Energy, Not Just Time

Introduction: The Hidden Power of Energy Management

In the modern business landscape, much of the emphasis is placed on time management—the need to squeeze more tasks into a day, organize schedules with military precision, and remain highly productive throughout the workweek. While time management is certainly important, it often overlooks a critical component of sustained success: energy management. For many introverted entrepreneurs, leaders, and professionals, the focus on time often leads to burnout, exhaustion, and a lack of creative focus. Simply put, managing your time effectively doesn't mean much if you don't have the energy to execute the work in a way that brings true value.

This chapter will explore the importance of energy management and how understanding and managing your energy can have a profound impact on your ability to do deep work, engage in creative pursuits, and prevent burnout. We'll cover strategies to help introverts manage their mental and physical energy, create workweek schedules that align with natural energy rhythms, and understand the importance of social recovery time as an essential part of maintaining mental and emotional health.

Energy management is not about squeezing more work into less time; it's about creating the conditions in which you can work at your highest level of focus and creativity, all while protecting your well-being. Let's dive into how managing energy, not just time, can help you achieve more with less stress, maintain a sustainable pace, and foster true productivity.

1. Energy Management Strategies for Deep Work and Creative Focus

The Importance of Deep Work

Our world is filled with distractions—endless notifications, emails, social media updates, and interruptions—true focus has become a rare and valuable commodity. For introverts, however, the ability to focus deeply on important work can be a superpower. Introverts tend to thrive in environments where they can engage in deep work, which is the ability to focus on complex tasks that require intense concentration and creativity. This might include writing, coding, designing, or solving intricate problems.

The challenge, though, is that deep work requires a lot of mental energy, and sustaining this type of focus over long periods is difficult without the proper strategies for energy management. Unlike time, which can be measured in hours and minutes, energy is more intangible but equally crucial. Energy levels fluctuate throughout the day, and understanding how to align your work with your energy patterns can drastically improve your ability to stay productive without feeling drained.

Maximizing Deep Work Through Energy Awareness

Introverts often do their best work when they can dive deep into projects without interruptions. To effectively manage energy for deep work, introverts should consider the following strategies:

- **Identify Your Peak Energy Periods**: One of the most important aspects of energy management is understanding when you have the most mental energy during the day. Many introverts find that they have the most energy and focus during the morning or early afternoon. This is when they can engage in deep work and make the most progress on challenging tasks. By scheduling your most important work during these periods, you can accomplish more while using less energy.

- **Time Blocking for Deep Work**: Time blocking is a technique that involves dedicating specific periods of your day to certain tasks. For introverts, time blocking can be especially helpful for ensuring that deep work happens without distractions. Use your peak energy periods to schedule uninterrupted time for creative tasks. During these blocks, focus on one task at a time, eliminate distractions, and immerse yourself fully in the work.

- **Taking Breaks to Replenish Energy**: While deep work requires focus, it also requires regular breaks to maintain energy levels. Introverts may find that after a period of intense concentration, they need time to recharge. Incorporating short breaks throughout the day—whether it's a walk outside, a meditation session, or a few minutes of stretching—can prevent mental fatigue and keep energy levels high throughout the day.

- **Setting Boundaries Around Work**: Another critical strategy for energy management is setting boundaries around work to prevent burnout. Introverts often feel drained by constant demands from others, whether it's from meetings, emails, or client interactions. By setting clear boundaries, you can protect your energy for the tasks that matter most, while also ensuring that you have time to recover and recharge.

Real-life example:

- **Cal Newport**, the author of "Deep Work", advocates for deep work and the importance of focusing on cognitively demanding tasks without distractions. Newport has built a career on the principle of deep work, and he shares in his book how he organizes his workday around periods of focused, uninterrupted work. His strategy for deep work, which includes scheduling large chunks of undisturbed time, has helped him stay productive while maintaining high levels of focus and creativity.

2. Designing Your Workweek to Prevent Burnout

Understanding the Energy Drains of a Typical Workweek

Traditional workweeks—where employees are expected to work 40 or more hours, often without sufficient breaks—can quickly lead to burnout, especially for introverts. The constant demands, deadlines, meetings, and social interactions drain mental and emotional energy, making it difficult to sustain focus and creativity. For introverts, working long hours without sufficient time for social recovery or recharging can be particularly taxing.

To avoid burnout, it's essential to design a workweek that aligns with your energy levels, rather than one that simply fills up time with tasks and obligations. By understanding when you are most likely to feel drained and when you are most productive, you can create a schedule that maximizes your energy while also allowing for recovery.

Creating a Balanced Workweek for Introverts

Introverts can benefit from designing a workweek that follows these guidelines:

- **Balance High-Energy and Low-Energy Tasks**: Plan your workweek by aligning your most demanding tasks (like deep work, strategic planning, or creative projects) with your peak energy periods. When your energy is high, tackle the most challenging tasks. During low-energy times, focus on less mentally demanding tasks, such as responding to emails, organizing files, or doing administrative work. This balance ensures you conserve your energy for the most important tasks.

- **Incorporate Downtime Between Tasks**: Introverts often need time between high-energy activities to recharge. For example, after a long meeting or an intense period of deep work, introverts may need 15–20 minutes of quiet time to regain focus and energy.

Schedule mini-breaks between tasks to allow for recovery and avoid mental fatigue.

- **Work in Focused Blocks**: To maintain energy throughout the week, introverts may find it helpful to work in focused time blocks, such as the Pomodoro Technique, where you work intensely for 25 minutes and then take a 5-minute break. Working in focused blocks can help prevent burnout while ensuring that tasks are completed efficiently.

- **Avoid Over-scheduling**: Many introverts feel overwhelmed by a packed schedule that requires constant social interaction, meetings, and phone calls. To prevent this, limit your meetings and scheduling so that you have ample time for independent work, reflection, and recovery. This allows you to focus on tasks that align with your strengths and ensures that your workweek remains manageable.

- **Schedule Time for Reflection and Planning**: Introverts often thrive when they have time for reflection and strategic thinking. Plan regular periods during your week for reviewing your goals, reflecting on your progress, and adjusting your plans as necessary. This time allows you to stay aligned with your values and vision while avoiding decision fatigue.

Real-life example:

- **Elon Musk**, the CEO of **Tesla** and **SpaceX**, is known for his intense work schedule, but he also follows strict routines to ensure that he stays productive while managing his energy. Musk breaks his day into five-minute blocks, which allows him to prioritize high-energy tasks and avoid burnout. Although his schedule is demanding, his ability to prioritize deep work and minimize distractions is central to his productivity.

3. Social Recovery Time: Why It's Not a Luxury

The Importance of Social Recovery for Introverts

While introverts tend to excel in solitary, deep work environments, they still need social interactions to thrive. However, unlike extroverts who gain energy from socializing, introverts often find social interactions to be energy-draining, especially if they involve large groups or extended periods of time. For introverts, social recovery is just as important as work recovery.

Introverts need to spend time alone or in low-stimulation environments to recharge their mental and emotional batteries. This is crucial for maintaining energy levels and ensuring that you can continue to be productive and effective without experiencing burnout.

Creating a Social Recovery Plan

To ensure that you have the energy to manage both work and social commitments, introverts should create a social recovery plan:

- **Set Boundaries Around Social Events**: For introverts, it's important to set clear boundaries around social commitments. You don't have to attend every meeting or gathering—be selective about the events that align with your goals and values.

If you do attend social events, ensure that you have scheduled recovery time afterward to recharge.

- **Plan Quiet Activities**: After a busy workday or social event, plan quiet activities that allow you to recharge. Whether it's reading, walking, journaling, or meditating, these activities help calm your mind and restore your energy.

- **Engage in Meaningful Social Interactions**: Instead of attending large social events that drain your energy, introverts can opt for smaller, more intimate gatherings with close friends or colleagues. These interactions allow for deeper connections and less energy expenditure compared to large groups or noisy environments.

- **Prioritize Alone Time**: Make sure to schedule regular solo time in your week, where you can retreat from the demands of work and social life. This time is essential for self-reflection, creative thinking, and simply recharging your emotional and mental energy.

Conclusion: Mastering Energy for Sustainable Success

Managing energy, not just time, is the key to achieving long-term success without sacrificing well-being. Introverts, by nature, have the ability to manage their energy effectively, but they must also learn to prioritize recovery, reflection, and self-care. By understanding your energy patterns, creating a balanced workweek, and ensuring that you have enough social recovery time, you can achieve the high levels of productivity and creativity that come with managing energy rather than simply time.

With these strategies in place, you can create a sustainable work routine that allows you to produce high-quality work, stay engaged with your business, and avoid burnout. By managing your energy in a strategic way, you will be able to maintain focus, enhance creativity, and lead a successful business while preserving your mental and emotional health.

Chapter 9

Networking for the Quiet Soul

Introduction: The Quiet Power of Meaningful Connections

For many introverts and quiet individuals, the idea of networking can seem daunting. In a world where success is often associated with socializing, attending events, and constantly interacting with new people, introverts may feel like they're at a disadvantage. The very thought of networking, traditionally seen as a noisy, extroverted activity, can cause feelings of discomfort or overwhelm. Yet, in the modern business world, networking is a crucial part of success. The difference is that meaningful networking—one built on authentic relationships and shared values—can be done without constant small talk or high-pressure socializing.

In this chapter, we'll explore how introverts can build a meaningful network without feeling the need to perform or engage in superficial conversations. Instead of pushing yourself to participate in every social event or trying to win over people with forced interactions, we will focus on strategic networking that feels authentic, aligns with your values, and allows you to build real, lasting relationships.

Networking doesn't have to be about collecting business cards or shaking as many hands as possible. It can be about building quality connections with like-minded individuals, engaging in meaningful conversations, and cultivating relationships that provide value to both you and the people you connect with. Quiet networking, when done right, allows you to grow your business and career without burning out or compromising your introverted nature.

1. How to Build a Meaningful Network Without Constant Small Talk

The Dread of Small Talk

Small talk, the casual and often superficial exchange of pleasantries, can be a major barrier for introverts when it comes to networking. It can feel inauthentic, draining, and purposeless. For many introverts, the idea of engaging in meaningless chatter to simply fill the silence feels uncomfortable and counterproductive. The pressure to "network" in traditional, loud settings—like large events, parties, or corporate mixers—can leave introverts feeling exhausted and disconnected.

However, effective networking doesn't require you to participate in small talk or fake enthusiasm about topics that don't interest you. Instead, introverts can build their networks around genuine relationships by focusing on deeper conversations and cultivating connections that have long-term value.

Strategic Networking vs. Networking for the Sake of It

For introverts, the key to successful networking lies in quality over quantity. Instead of aiming to meet as many people as possible, focus on building meaningful relationships with a select few who share your values, interests, and goals. This strategic networking can happen in a variety of ways, including one-on-one meetings, focused discussions, and online engagement.

Instead of pushing yourself to attend every event or meeting every person in the room, take a more thoughtful approach to networking by:

- **Setting clear intentions** for your networking efforts.

- **Focusing on building long-term relationships** rather than immediate returns.

- **Engaging in deep conversations** that align with your professional interests and passions.

Real-life example:

- **Bill Gates**, co-founder of Microsoft, is often described as a quiet and introverted leader who built an extraordinary network through thoughtful connections and meaningful relationships rather than frequent socializing. Gates has shared how his preferred method of networking involves deep, one-on-one conversations with key individuals, rather than attending large events or seeking to network with as many people as possible. His ability to focus on quality relationships has played a crucial role in his success and the growth of his philanthropic efforts.

Building Relationships Through Shared Values

The foundation of meaningful networking lies in building relationships with people who share your values, passions, and vision. Networking for introverts isn't about chasing superficial connections or accumulating a large contact list. Instead, it's about forming bonds with people who genuinely resonate with your work, your goals, and your vision for the future. These relationships are more likely to be mutually beneficial and sustainable in the long run.

To build relationships based on shared values, consider the following strategies:

- **Engage with people in your field**: Instead of attending large, unrelated networking events, seek out smaller, niche communities that align with your interests and expertise. These communities provide a more intimate setting where you can connect with others who share your passions and values.

- **Focus on giving before receiving**: Introverts often excel at listening and empathizing with others. Use this to your advantage by offering value first—whether through advice, resources, or genuine support. By being helpful and generous, you lay the foundation for a relationship built on trust and mutual respect.

- **Stay consistent**: Building strong relationships takes time. Introverts tend to excel at forming deep, long-lasting connections because they invest in people over the long term. Regular check-ins, follow-ups, and offering support when needed are all ways to show that you care and are committed to the relationship.

2. Strategic Online Networking

Leveraging Social Media for Introverts

In today's digital world, online networking presents a powerful opportunity for introverts to connect with others without the pressure of face-to-face interactions. Platforms such as LinkedIn, Twitter, Facebook, and Instagram provide valuable spaces for introverts to showcase their expertise, engage with like-minded individuals, and build a community— all from the comfort of their own home.

For introverts, online networking allows them to interact at their own pace, responding thoughtfully rather than feeling pressured to engage in spontaneous conversations. Here are several strategies for strategic online networking:

- **Define your online presence**: Craft a clear and concise online profile that reflects your values, expertise, and goals. Focus on providing value through your posts, articles, or comments, and position yourself as a trusted resource in your field. By clearly articulating your expertise and vision, you attract connections that align with your interests and goals.

- **Join online communities**: Instead of attending large, impersonal networking events, seek out small, niche communities related to your field. These could be LinkedIn groups, industry-specific forums, or professional associations. Engage meaningfully with other members by offering thoughtful comments, sharing resources, and initiating discussions that contribute to the community.

- **Create valuable content**: Share your knowledge and insights by creating content that adds value to your audience. This could include blog posts, videos, podcasts, or social media updates. By sharing your expertise in a non-salesy way, you build trust and credibility while connecting with potential collaborators, clients, or mentors.

The Power of Authentic Online Connections

One of the key advantages of online networking is that it allows you to connect with people who share your interests and values regardless of geographic location. Introverts often thrive in environments where they can connect one-on-one with others and engage in deep, meaningful conversations. Online networking allows introverts to build relationships based on authenticity, rather than relying on small talk or superficial exchanges.

Real-life example:

- **Sophia Amoruso**, the founder of Nasty Gal and the author of the book #GIRLBOSS, used social media as a powerful tool to build her brand and connect with her audience. By being authentic and vulnerable in her online presence, she was able to create a community of supporters who felt personally connected to her journey. Amoruso's ability to build relationships online, through genuine engagement rather than flashy marketing, helped her create a brand that resonated deeply with her audience.

3. Thoughtful Relationship-Building Over Hustle

The Cost of the Hustle Culture

In today's hyper-competitive business environment, there is a prevailing narrative around the "hustle culture"—the idea that success requires constant networking, grinding, and overwork. The focus on quantity rather than quality has led many to believe that in order to succeed, they need to be constantly seeking new connections, attending every networking event, and chasing the next opportunity. However, this approach often leads to burnout, shallow relationships, and a lack of authenticity.

For introverts, the hustle culture can feel particularly draining. Introverts thrive in meaningful connections rather than superficial exchanges, and the idea of constantly hustling can feel disconnected from their values. Building thoughtful relationships, however, allows introverts to forge deeper connections with those who genuinely resonate with their vision and expertise. This approach fosters collaboration, respect, and trust, all while avoiding the overwhelming pressure of hustle culture.

Building Meaningful Relationships Over Time

Building a successful business network isn't about how many people you know, but about how many meaningful relationships you have. Introverts excel at creating lasting relationships based on mutual understanding, shared values, and collaboration. Rather than aiming for instant gratification or quick wins, introverts focus on cultivating long-term relationships that evolve over time.

Key strategies for building thoughtful relationships include:

- **Investing time in fewer, deeper connections**: Instead of spreading yourself thin by trying to network with as many people as possible, focus on building a smaller number of genuine connections. Be strategic in choosing those you invest in and develop those relationships over time.

- **Follow-up with intention**: Introverts excel at following up with people in meaningful ways. After meeting someone, send a thoughtful follow-up message or email that adds value. Acknowledge the conversation, share something useful, or offer help where possible. This thoughtful approach leaves a lasting impression and shows that you care about building a meaningful connection rather than just networking for business.

Conclusion: Quiet Networking as a Strength

For introverts, networking doesn't have to be a high-energy, performative task. By focusing on building genuine relationships, leveraging strategic online networking, and creating meaningful connections, introverts can network effectively without compromising their values or energy levels. Networking with authenticity, empathy, and thoughtfulness allows introverts to build a powerful network that supports their business and professional goals while remaining true to who they are.

In a world that often prioritizes loud, extroverted behaviors, introverts have a unique opportunity to build a network based on quality and connection, rather than quantity and hype. Through intentional networking, introverts can create a space where they feel comfortable, respected, and energized, building relationships that foster both personal and professional growth.

PART IV
SCALING WITH EASE AND INTEGRITY

Chapter 10

Thought Leadership, the Introvert Way

Introduction: The Quiet Power of Thought Leadership

In today's fast-paced, digital world, thought leadership has become an essential way for entrepreneurs, leaders, and business owners to establish themselves as experts in their fields. However, for introverts, the idea of thought leadership may seem intimidating, particularly when it's associated with public speaking, constant self-promotion, or a loud presence in the marketplace. It's easy to assume that to be a successful thought leader, one must always be at the forefront, leading workshops, giving keynote speeches, and dominating social media platforms.

However, introverts have a unique advantage when it comes to thought leadership: the ability to lead through quiet influence. Rather than relying on loud proclamations, introverts excel at leading through introspection, deep thinking, and meaningful content. For introverted leaders, being a thought leader doesn't require shouting to be heard. Instead, it's about being consistent, deliberate, and authentic in your content creation, and allowing your expertise to shine through long-term value.

In this chapter, we will explore how introverts can become go-to experts in their industries and build their influence without the need for loud or extroverted behaviors. We'll dive into the power of blogging, podcasting, and long-form content as tools for introverts to share their ideas, connect with their audience, and build a legacy of thought leadership. Furthermore, we'll discuss how the compound effect of consistent, quiet content can establish introverts as trusted voices in their fields, allowing them to lead with integrity and insight, rather than relying on flashy marketing tactics or self-promotion.

By the end of this chapter, you will have a clear understanding of how to build your thought leadership as an introvert, leveraging your quiet strengths to create an authentic, lasting influence in your industry.

1. Becoming a Go-To Expert Without Shouting

What is Thought Leadership?

Thought leadership is about positioning yourself as a trusted authority in your field, sharing insights and ideas that provide value to others, and influencing people's thinking in a way that sparks positive change. Being a thought leader doesn't mean you have to be the loudest voice in the room; it means that you have developed deep expertise in your area and are willing to share it with others in a way that helps them grow, learn, and solve problems.

For introverts, thought leadership may not look like the typical, extroverted version—dominating social media feeds with constant updates, or hosting live events to grab attention. Instead, introverts are more inclined to influence through thoughtful, considered content that speaks to their audience in an authentic, deep, and deliberate way.

Introverts can become thought leaders by:

- **Sharing expertise through content creation**: Writing articles, blog posts, or books, creating podcasts or video series—these are all ways introverts can share their knowledge and establish themselves as experts in their field.

- **Engaging in one-on-one mentorship**: Introverts excel in personalized, deep conversations. Providing mentorship or coaching can be a powerful way to establish thought leadership without the need for large groups or public events.

- **Building an online presence**: Introverts can create a platform where their ideas can flourish and reach a wide audience— whether it's a personal blog, a LinkedIn profile, or an industry-specific forum. Through consistent, valuable contributions, introverts can cultivate a reputation as an expert without forcing visibility.

Real-life example:

- **Seth Godin**, a well-known marketing expert and author, is an excellent example of a thought leader who has built his influence quietly through writing and creating valuable content. Rather than relying on public speaking or flashy self-promotion, Godin has built his career on his blog and books. His content, consistently thoughtful and deep, has earned him a dedicated following of entrepreneurs and business professionals who value his insights on marketing, leadership, and creativity.

Leading with Quiet Authority

As an introvert, you may prefer to lead from behind the scenes, offering insight when needed and allowing your expertise to speak for itself. In the world of thought leadership, quiet authority is often more powerful than loud self-promotion. Being an introvert does not mean you lack authority or influence; it simply means your leadership style is likely to be more reflective, intentional, and subtle.

By cultivating quiet authority, you can build your thought leadership around the concept of authenticity rather than performance. When introverts embrace their natural approach to leadership—emphasizing calm, reflection, and deep thinking—they develop a unique leadership style that resonates with others and draws people in.

Key qualities of quiet authority:

- **Authenticity**: Introverts can be authentic in their thoughts, ideas, and actions, which builds trust and credibility.

- **Deep listening**: Introverts often excel at listening deeply to others, which fosters a deeper connection and allows them to share ideas that truly address the needs of their audience.

- **Consistency**: Quiet leaders maintain a steady presence and are known for their reliability, which earns them respect over time.

- **Patience**: Introverts can be patient in developing relationships, cultivating their influence gradually without the pressure to rush or perform.

Real-life example:

- **Malala Yousafzai,** the Nobel Peace Prize-winning activist, has become a global thought leader in the areas of education and women's rights, particularly for young girls in underserved areas. Despite being young and soft-spoken, her consistent message, authentic advocacy, and quiet resilience have earned her influence worldwide. Her leadership is based on her commitment to a cause and her ability to speak with authority on issues that matter, despite not raising her voice or seeking the limelight.

2. Blogging, Podcasting, and Long-Form Content as Tools of Influence

Blogging: The Power of Written Thought Leadership

One of the most powerful tools for introverts to establish themselves as thought leaders is through blogging. Writing allows introverts to express themselves clearly, at their own pace, and without the pressure of being on display. Blogging provides the time and space to develop deep insights and share valuable content that helps others while simultaneously establishing expertise.

Blogging is also an excellent way for introverts to connect with their audience over time. Unlike social media, which tends to be fast-paced and short-lived, blogs offer long-term content that remains relevant for years. When you write consistently and thoughtfully, your ideas can accumulate, establishing you as a trusted resource in your industry.

Some ways to leverage blogging for thought leadership:

- **Create evergreen content**: Write blog posts that answer common questions, offer solutions, and provide lasting value. Over time, these posts will continue to bring in traffic and lead to greater recognition.

- **Share personal stories and experiences**: Introverts often have unique perspectives shaped by their thoughtfulness and reflective nature. Share your experiences, challenges, and lessons learned in a way that resonates with your audience.

- **Offer insights based on research**: As an introvert, you may enjoy deep research and reflection. Use this to your advantage by publishing in-depth articles that showcase your expertise and provide value to your audience.

Real-life example:

- **Tim Ferriss**, the author of *The 4-Hour Workweek*, has built his thought leadership through his blog and podcast. Ferriss shares personal experiences, interviews with experts, and deep dives into topics related to productivity, business, and lifestyle. His blog has become a go-to resource for aspiring entrepreneurs, demonstrating how blogging can be an effective tool for introverts to establish authority.

Podcasting: Voice as a Tool for Thought Leadership

Another excellent tool for introverts is podcasting. While podcasting might seem like an extroverted activity, introverts have a unique advantage in this format. Unlike video, podcasting is low-pressure and allows for in-depth conversation without the need for constant visual engagement. It's the perfect medium for introverts who want to share their insights, experiences, and knowledge with a larger audience while maintaining an authentic, low-key presence.

Podcasting allows for consistent engagement with your audience, and over time, it establishes you as a trusted voice in your field. Introverts can use podcasts to:

- **Dive deep into topics**: Use the time to explore complex subjects and offer value to your audience.

- **Interview experts**: Podcasting offers the opportunity to engage with experts in your field, allowing you to build relationships and share those conversations with your audience.

- **Showcase your personality**: Without the visual distractions of video, podcasting allows listeners to connect with you on a personal level, helping them understand your thoughts, perspectives, and expertise.

Real-life example:

- **Brene Brown**, the research professor and author, has built a massive following through her podcast, Unlocking Us, where she interviews experts on topics related to vulnerability, courage, and leadership. Brown's soft-spoken and empathetic approach makes her podcast a valuable resource, showing that introverts can leverage the power of voice to lead and inspire.

3. The Compound Effect of Consistent Quiet Thought Leadership

Consistency is Key

One of the greatest strengths of introverted thought leadership is the compound effect of consistent effort. Introverts may not be able to build influence overnight, but with steady, thoughtful contributions over time, they can become trusted voices in their fields. The compound effect is about small, consistent actions that, when repeated over time, lead to exponential growth in influence, recognition, and authority.

For introverts, this means committing to regular content creation, whether it's blogging, podcasting, writing articles, or engaging on social media. As you build content that consistently provides value to your audience, you will slowly build your influence, one interaction at a time. Your voice will become stronger, and your ideas will spread further.

Building a Legacy of Quiet Influence

The beauty of introverted thought leadership is that it doesn't have to be flashy or loud to be impactful. In fact, the most profound leadership often comes from those who operate in the background, quietly guiding others with their ideas, expertise, and integrity. By creating consistent, high-quality content and building authentic relationships, introverts can leave a lasting legacy that is based on trust, value, and authenticity.

Conclusion: Quiet Thought Leadership as a Lasting Influence

Introverts have the ability to lead and influence with quiet strength. Through blogging, podcasting, and long-form content, introverts can build powerful thought leadership that resonates with others and leaves a lasting impact. By focusing on quality over quantity, authentic connections, and the compound effect of consistent contributions, introverts can establish themselves as experts in their fields without ever having to raise their voices.

The key to becoming a thought leader as an introvert is to embrace your natural strengths—deep thinking, authenticity, and calm reflection—and use them to create content and relationships that build trust over time. Thought leadership, when done quietly, is one of the most powerful ways introverts can make a lasting mark on the world.

Chapter 11

Building a Loyal Audience Without the Spotlight

Introduction: The Power of Quiet Influence

In today's fast-paced, digital-first world, it's easy to feel pressured to constantly be in the spotlight in order to gain visibility and build a successful business. Social media is often flooded with influencers shouting for attention, entrepreneurs promoting themselves, and content creators posting incessantly to stay relevant. For introverts, this type of high-energy engagement can feel overwhelming and inauthentic. The common perception that success requires being in the limelight often leaves those with quieter, more reflective approaches questioning their ability to build a thriving audience.

However, as an introvert, you possess a unique strength that can be leveraged to create a loyal, engaged audience without the need for constant visibility or self-promotion. Building a loyal audience without the spotlight means focusing on authenticity, resonance, and sustained engagement rather than chasing numbers or competing for attention. It's about cultivating a small-but-mighty community that genuinely connects with your message, values, and vision.

In this chapter, we will explore how to build a loyal audience that isn't based on flash or temporary attention, but on the lasting connections you form through authenticity, consistent value, and real engagement. We will dive into the strategies you can use to cultivate a community that respects your voice, aligns with your values, and continues to engage without the need for constant, high-visibility activity.

1. Cultivating a Small-but-Mighty Community

The Value of Smaller, More Focused Communities

One of the most effective ways for introverts to build a loyal audience is by cultivating a small-but-mighty community. The idea of having a large audience can seem appealing, but the truth is that a smaller, engaged community can often lead to far more meaningful interactions, deeper connections, and long-term success.

Why smaller communities matter:

- **Stronger connections**: In a smaller community, members are more likely to feel heard and understood. They have more opportunities to engage with you directly, and you have the time and energy to build genuine relationships with each member. This creates a sense of trust and loyalty that is difficult to achieve in larger, more impersonal communities.

- **Higher engagement**: Smaller communities tend to have higher engagement rates because members are more invested in the group and its purpose. With fewer people, it's easier to maintain authentic conversations, provide personalized feedback, and create a space where everyone feels like they belong.

- **Better feedback**: When you have a smaller audience, you are more likely to receive meaningful feedback that helps you improve your content, products, or services. You'll have the chance to fine-tune your offerings based on real insights from people who truly care about your work.

- **Long-term relationships**: Introverts often excel at building strong, long-term relationships rather than temporary connections. In smaller communities, these relationships have the space to grow organically, creating a core group of followers who will remain loyal to you over time, even as your business evolves.

Rather than trying to appeal to everyone or grow your audience as quickly as possible, focus on nurturing the people who are most likely to resonate with your message and become advocates for your work. You don't need to have tens of thousands of followers to create impact— what matters is the **quality** of the relationships you build and the depth of your community's engagement.

Real-life example:

- **Marie Forleo**, an entrepreneur and author, is a great example of someone who has built a small but mighty community. Forleo's B-School is a well-established online business program, but rather than focusing on attracting huge numbers of people, she has cultivated a loyal following of entrepreneurs who deeply connect with her message. Her community is engaged, loyal, and actively participates in her work, creating a sustainable and supportive environment that doesn't require constant attention-grabbing efforts.

2. Leveraging Authenticity and Resonance Over Reach

Authenticity as the Core of Connection

Authenticity is the cornerstone of building a loyal audience. In a world full of polished, performative content, the ability to be real and share your true self is what sets you apart. Authenticity attracts people who resonate with your message, values, and vision. They are drawn to you not because of your ability to sell or promote, but because of the genuine connection you foster.

Introverts often excel at being authentic because they tend to be introspective, thoughtful, and intentional in their approach. Instead of trying to cater to a broad audience or fitting into a specific mold, introverts can embrace their unique voice and attract those who align with their message.

Resonance Over Reach

While many businesses focus on growing their audience numbers, introverts can gain a distinct advantage by focusing on resonance over reach. Resonance means creating content that truly speaks to your audience, engages their hearts and minds, and builds trust over time. Instead of chasing reach and vanity metrics (like follower counts or views), prioritize building deeper connections with those who truly resonate with what you're offering.

Key strategies for leveraging authenticity and resonance:

- **Share your personal story**: People connect with stories, and introverts often have rich, meaningful narratives that can inspire others. Sharing your journey, struggles, and triumphs allows your audience to see you as relatable and authentic.

- **Focus on quality over quantity**: Rather than trying to reach as many people as possible, focus on creating content that provides real value to your core audience. Deep, well-thought-out content is more likely to resonate than superficial, quick hits.

- **Engage thoughtfully with your audience**: Take the time to respond to comments, answer questions, and show up for your community. Introverts excel at thoughtful interactions, so use this to your advantage by being intentional in your engagement. A personal reply or a meaningful comment can go a long way in building genuine relationships.

- **Be transparent and vulnerable**: Authenticity often requires vulnerability. Don't be afraid to share your struggles, challenges, or even mistakes. When you show your true self, your audience will feel more connected and trust you even more.

Real-life example:

- **Brene Brown**, a well-known researcher and author, has built an incredibly loyal following by focusing on authenticity. Her work on vulnerability and shame resonates deeply with her audience because she openly shares her own experiences and challenges.

Brown has built an engaged community of followers who feel connected to her message and who trust her guidance. Her ability to be authentic in her work has made her one of the most respected thought leaders today.

3. Engagement Without Constant Presence

The Challenge of Constant Availability

One of the most difficult aspects of traditional networking and social media engagement is the constant pressure to be available and active. For many introverts, this need for continuous interaction can lead to burnout and frustration. It may feel like you are expected to be constantly present in order to keep your audience engaged, but this is not sustainable for introverts who need time alone to recharge.

Instead of relying on constant interaction, introverts can use strategic engagement to stay connected with their audience without the need for nonstop presence. The goal is to engage meaningfully, but not exhaust yourself by always being "on."

Creating Consistent, Value-Driven Content

The key to engagement without constant presence is creating value-driven content that can work for you while you rest and recharge. By batching content in advance and using tools like social media schedulers, you can stay present with your audience without needing to be constantly active. Focus on providing your audience with content that speaks to their needs, adds value, and builds trust over time.

For example, consider creating a content calendar that allows you to plan your content in advance, whether that's blog posts, videos, or social media updates. With thoughtful planning, you can ensure that your audience continues to receive valuable insights and updates, even when you're not actively posting.

The Power of Scheduling "Social Recovery" Time

While engagement is important, so is self-care. Introverts often need time to recover after social interactions or periods of public engagement. Scheduling "social recovery" time is essential for maintaining your energy levels and preventing burnout. This time can be used for reflection, personal activities, or creative pursuits, allowing you to regain your energy and come back stronger for your audience.

Real-life example:

- **Gary Vaynerchuk**, a successful entrepreneur and thought leader, is known for his high-energy social media presence and engagement. However, Vaynerchuk has built a team and a content strategy that allows him to be strategically engaged while still maintaining time for himself. His content, which includes blog posts, videos, and social media updates, is carefully planned and scheduled to ensure consistent engagement without requiring constant real-time interaction.

Conclusion: Building a Legacy of Quiet Influence

Networking and building an audience does not have to be about constant presence, loud engagement, or endless self-promotion. For introverts, the power lies in creating a small but mighty community that resonates deeply with your message, values, and vision. Through authenticity, consistency, and strategic engagement, introverts can cultivate a loyal following that is built on trust and shared value rather than shallow interactions.

By focusing on quality connections over quantity, creating evergreen content that continues to engage over time, and scheduling social recovery to protect your energy, introverts can build a sustainable and impactful audience. The quiet power of introverted networking lies in your ability to foster deep, meaningful relationships, show up authentically, and create content that continues to work for you long after it's been published. Through these efforts, you can build a network that supports your business, fosters personal growth, and allows you to lead without the need for constant visibility.

Chapter 12

Collaborating Without Losing Yourself

Introduction: The Art of Collaboration for Introverts

In today's collaborative and fast-paced business environment, partnerships and collaborations are often seen as key drivers of success. As an introvert, the idea of working closely with extroverts, influencers, or media outlets may seem both appealing and intimidating. While collaboration can open doors to greater visibility, opportunities, and growth, it can also come with challenges, particularly for those who thrive on solitude and quiet reflection.

Introverts often have a natural inclination to work independently, where they can control their environment, pace, and focus. However, in a world that increasingly values networking, teamwork, and visibility, introverts are often faced with the dilemma of how to collaborate without compromising their energy, well-being, or personal work style. The good news is that collaboration doesn't have to drain you. By setting clear boundaries, maintaining your authentic approach to work, and knowing when to say no to the wrong opportunities, introverts can build fruitful partnerships that allow them to grow their influence without sacrificing their personal peace or energy.

This chapter will explore how introverts can successfully collaborate with extroverts, influencers, and media outlets while preserving their core energy and work style. We'll dive into practical strategies for setting boundaries, maintaining authenticity, and discerning when an opportunity aligns with your goals and when it's best to pass on it. Collaboration can be empowering and energizing, even for introverts, as long as it is done with intention and mindfulness.

1. Partnering with Extroverts, Influencers, or Media Without Draining Your Energy

The Power of Introvert-Extrovert Partnerships

One of the most valuable aspects of collaboration is working with people whose strengths complement your own. Extroverts, influencers, and media personalities often bring a dynamic energy to a project, with their ability to network, engage with large audiences, and think outside the box. These qualities can be a great complement to the thoughtful, focused, and introspective approach that many introverts bring to the table. However, collaborating with extroverts or media personalities also requires navigating the differences in energy levels and work styles.

For introverts, working with extroverts can be an opportunity to expand their reach without needing to push themselves to perform in ways that feel uncomfortable. Extroverts tend to thrive on high-energy environments, frequent interactions, and visible results, while introverts excel at creating thoughtful, well-crafted work. The key to a successful partnership is understanding and respecting these differences, and finding ways to leverage each other's strengths.

Key Strategies for Introverts in Collaborative Partnerships

- **Set Clear Expectations from the Start**: When partnering with extroverts or influencers, it's important to have an open conversation about roles, expectations, and boundaries. For example, if an extrovert partner is more comfortable with public-facing tasks like social media or interviews, you can set the expectation that your role will focus on content creation, strategy, or behind-the-scenes work. Clarifying expectations helps prevent misunderstandings and ensures that each partner can focus on their strengths.

- **Balance Public Exposure with Private Time**: Introverts often find that public-facing tasks such as social media promotion, public speaking, or live events can be draining. In collaborations with extroverts or media, it's important to negotiate a balance. For example, you might agree to participate in interviews or media appearances, but only on your terms—perhaps through pre-recorded formats rather than live events, or limiting the number of engagements to avoid social burnout.

- **Leverage Technology for Seamless Collaboration**: Technology can be a lifesaver for introverts when collaborating with extroverts or influencers. Online communication platforms, project management tools, and virtual meetings allow introverts to collaborate without needing to be constantly present or engaged in high-energy settings. Introverts can focus on writing, editing, or strategic thinking, while their extroverted counterparts handle live engagement, media outreach, or audience interaction.

Real-life example:

- **Marie Forleo**, an introverted entrepreneur, has successfully built her brand and business by collaborating with high-energy influencers, like Tony Robbins and other motivational speakers. While Forleo's strength lies in content creation, strategy, and thought leadership, she partners with extroverts who bring additional energy and visibility to her projects. Through clear communication and a strategic balance of roles, Forleo has been able to create a sustainable and harmonious partnership that allows both parties to thrive.

2. Setting Boundaries and Preserving Your Work Style

Why Boundaries Matter

Introverts often struggle with the pressure to say yes to every opportunity that arises. The fear of missing out or being left behind can create anxiety around saying no. However, setting clear boundaries is essential for introverts to preserve their energy and maintain their authentic work style. Boundaries are not about being rigid or inflexible; they are about ensuring that you can collaborate in ways that are sustainable and aligned with your personal values.

When you collaborate with others, it's easy to lose sight of your own needs, especially if the demands of the partnership begin to feel overwhelming. Boundaries help you prioritize your well-being and ensure that you can contribute your best work without sacrificing your personal peace.

Practical Tips for Setting Boundaries in Collaboration

- **Know Your Limits**: Before committing to a partnership, take the time to reflect on your energy levels and work style. How much time can you realistically dedicate to this collaboration without feeling burned out? What types of tasks drain you, and what types energize you? By understanding your limits upfront, you can make more informed decisions about what you're willing to take on.

- **Communicate Your Boundaries Early**: Open communication is key to maintaining healthy boundaries. If you need certain types of work to be done in specific ways (e.g., avoiding last-minute requests or needing time for reflection), communicate these needs clearly and respectfully from the beginning. Introverts often struggle with asserting their needs, but it's essential for maintaining a healthy work-life balance.

- **Create a Schedule that Supports Your Energy**: Introverts need to allocate recovery time into their schedules, especially when working with extroverts who may thrive on constant interaction. Whether that means scheduling quiet, solo time after collaborative meetings or ensuring that you have mental downtime after a busy work period, protecting your energy is key to maintaining a sustainable work style.

Real-life example:

- **Simon Sinek**, the leadership expert and author, is known for his methodical approach to work, which emphasizes clarity, purpose, and intentionality. Sinek is selective about the collaborations he takes on and has set boundaries around his time and energy to maintain his focus on his writing, speaking, and coaching. By saying no to opportunities that don't align with his values or energy levels, he's been able to sustain his impact over the long term without burning out.

3. Knowing When to Say No to "Big Opportunities"

The Temptation of "Big Opportunities"

As your network expands and your business grows, opportunities will inevitably come knocking—some of them promising massive exposure, lucrative deals, or career-changing prospects. For many introverts, the pressure to accept these opportunities can be overwhelming. The fear of missing out on something big or not being perceived as ambitious can make it difficult to say no.

However, the key to sustainable success lies in being able to evaluate opportunities through the lens of alignment rather than size. Just because an opportunity is big doesn't mean it's the right fit for you. In fact, pursuing opportunities that aren't aligned with your goals, values, or work style can lead to burnout and dissatisfaction.

How to Evaluate Opportunities and Know When to Say No

- **Assess Alignment with Your Values**: Before accepting any opportunity, take time to assess whether it aligns with your core values and vision for your business. Does this opportunity support your long-term goals? Does it resonate with your mission and message? If it feels out of alignment, it's okay to pass.

- **Understand the Cost of Taking On More**: Opportunities often come with hidden costs—time, energy, and emotional investment. Consider whether the opportunity will require you to sacrifice what you truly value or whether it will allow you to maintain your work-life balance. Will you be able to sustain this new collaboration without compromising your well-being or your business's integrity?

- **Trust Your Instincts**: Introverts are often highly intuitive and can rely on their gut feelings when evaluating opportunities. If something doesn't feel right or if the prospect of committing to it feels draining, trust your instincts and be okay with walking away.

Real-life example:

- **Oprah Winfrey** has built a massive media empire, but she has always been selective about the projects she takes on. Oprah's ability to say no to opportunities that didn't align with her personal values or the direction of her business allowed her to focus on creating meaningful content and building a brand based on authenticity and integrity.

Conclusion: Embracing Collaborative Success Without Sacrificing Yourself

Collaboration can be an invaluable tool for growth, but for introverts, it's essential to approach partnerships with a clear understanding of your own needs and boundaries. By partnering with extroverts, influencers, and media outlets in a way that leverages your quiet strengths, you can build meaningful collaborations that propel your business forward without compromising your energy or personal work style.

By setting clear boundaries, focusing on authentic partnerships, and knowing when to say no to opportunities that don't align with your values, introverts can create a path to success that feels genuine, sustainable, and empowering. Collaborating without losing yourself is about finding balance—working with others in ways that allow you to contribute your best while staying true to who you are and maintaining the energy needed to continue growing and thriving.

PART V
THE INNER WORK OF THE QUIET CLIMB

Chapter 13

Rewriting the Narrative – From "Too Quiet" to Powerful

Introduction: The Power of Quiet Strength

Throughout life, many introverts are often met with the same recurring narrative—"you're too quiet," or "you need to speak up more," or even "you're not outgoing enough to succeed." These messages, whether coming from peers, colleagues, or even well-meaning family members, are deeply ingrained in a culture that tends to equate outgoingness and extroversion with power, success, and leadership. But what if the opposite were true? What if being quiet, introverted, or reserved wasn't a weakness, but a profound strength? What if introverts could rewrite their personal and professional narratives and embrace the quiet power they possess?

In this chapter, we will explore how to reframe the narrative around introversion and turn past feedback or trauma related to your personality into a source of strength. We will discuss how to heal from the pressure to be more outgoing, reclaim your quiet confidence, and celebrate the unique advantages that introverts bring to the world of business, leadership, and life in general.

Through practical strategies, personal reflection, and real-life examples, this chapter will help you reclaim your identity as a quiet, powerful leader. By the end of this chapter, you will understand how to transform negative perceptions and embrace your authentic self, thriving as an introvert with quiet confidence, resilience, and power

1. Reframing Past Feedback or Trauma Around Your Personality

The Weight of External Expectations

From a young age, many introverts are often told to be "more social," "speak up more," or "engage with others" in ways that feel inauthentic to them. As introverts grow older and enter professional environments, these same messages persist. At work, introverts are sometimes overlooked for leadership opportunities, promotions, or projects, simply because their quiet demeanor is mistaken for a lack of leadership potential. This cultural narrative can create a sense of self-doubt, insecurity, and even trauma, leading many introverts to internalize the belief that something is wrong with them.

The first step in rewriting this narrative is to recognize the external expectations placed upon you and understand that they are often rooted in societal bias towards extroversion. These messages are not a reflection of your true potential or value but are influenced by outdated stereotypes about personality and success. By reframing these messages, you can begin to break free from the need for validation based on how loudly or outwardly you engage with the world.

Recognizing the Origin of the Narrative

To shift the narrative around introversion, start by examining the origins of your self-doubt. Think about the key moments in your life where you were told that you were "too quiet," "not outgoing enough," or "not assertive enough." Who said these things to you, and how did they shape your self-image? Often, these external judgments come from people who didn't understand your introverted nature or were influenced by societal norms that equate success with extroverted traits.

Take a moment to reflect on these moments:

- Did you receive feedback in school or work that made you feel like your quiet nature was something to be fixed?

- Were there moments when you held back from speaking up because you feared being perceived as too reserved or "shy"?

- Did past criticism from friends, family, or colleagues make you feel like you weren't being seen or valued for your contributions?

Recognizing the origin of these messages is the first step in reframing them. When you understand where these external pressures came from, you can separate them from your true self and challenge them with a new perspective. Instead of accepting them as truths, you can choose to see them as misunderstandings or biases that do not reflect your true potential.

Real-life example:

- **Albert Einstein**, widely regarded as one of the most influential minds in history, was often considered "too quiet" or "shy" in his early years. Teachers and peers thought he was disengaged or incapable of leadership because of his quiet nature. Yet, Einstein's introversion didn't hinder his ability to revolutionize the field of physics. In fact, his ability to think deeply and work independently was key to his success. His story shows how introverts can use their unique strengths to change the world, despite being misunderstood or underestimated in their earlier years.

2. Healing the Pressure to Be "More Outgoing"

The Myth of the Outgoing Leader

Society often places a great deal of emphasis on extroversion as the hallmark of successful leadership. The stereotypical image of a great leader is someone who is outgoing, charismatic, and enjoys engaging in social events and public speaking. But for introverts, this model can feel like an inherent mismatch, leading to frustration and self-doubt. Many introverts feel that they must adopt extroverted behaviors to succeed in business and leadership, but this is a false narrative.

The first step in healing from this pressure is to accept and embrace your introverted nature. Being introverted does not mean being weak, disengaged, or ineffective. On the contrary, introverts often excel in areas like strategic thinking, listening, and empathy—skills that are crucial for effective leadership and collaboration. Once you accept your introverted nature and stop trying to force yourself into an extroverted mold, you can begin to see your quiet traits as strengths.

Healing from the Pressure

To heal from the societal pressure to be more outgoing, consider the following steps:

- **Affirm your introverted strengths**: Take inventory of the qualities that make you a great leader. Introverts often excel at deep thinking, problem-solving, and one-on-one connections. By focusing on these strengths, you can shift the focus away from the pressure to "perform" and towards the value you bring to the table.

- **Give yourself permission to be quiet**: Healing begins with self-acceptance. Allow yourself to be the person you truly are without the need to meet external expectations. Being quiet is not a limitation—it's an opportunity to listen more deeply, think critically, and respond thoughtfully. Embrace your quiet nature as part of your leadership style.

- **Redefine leadership on your terms**: Leadership doesn't have to mean being the loudest or most outgoing person in the room. True leadership is about being able to inspire and guide others with clarity, vision, and purpose. As an introvert, you may be able to connect with your team or peers on a deeper level, offering guidance in a way that feels authentic and grounded.

Real-life example:

- **Barack Obama**, the 44th president of the United States, is often praised for his leadership style, which was grounded in thoughtfulness, calmness, and strategic vision. Obama, despite being considered introverted by many, used his quiet demeanor and reflective thinking to lead the nation through complex issues. His leadership is an example of how introverts can lead with power without being loud or extroverted.

3. Reclaiming Quiet Confidence

What is Quiet Confidence?

Quiet confidence is not about showing off, boasting, or seeking attention. It is about knowing your worth, trusting in your abilities, and being able to lead and make decisions with calm assurance. Quiet confidence is rooted in self-assurance and the ability to trust yourself and your intuition, without needing validation from others.

For introverts, reclaiming quiet confidence is about embracing the idea that you don't need to shout to be heard. Confidence doesn't require performance or exaggerated displays—it can be subtle, reserved, and powerful in its own way.

How to Reclaim Quiet Confidence

- **Recognize your achievements**: Quiet confidence begins with acknowledging your accomplishments. Reflect on the work you've done, the challenges you've overcome, and the growth you've experienced. This recognition of your past successes will reinforce your self-worth and help you feel more confident moving forward.

- **Trust your instincts**: Introverts are often highly intuitive and able to make decisions based on their deep thinking and reflection. Trusting your instincts and believing in your judgment can help you reclaim your confidence in both personal and professional situations.

- **Practice self-compassion**: Confidence comes from a place of self-love and self-acceptance. Stop beating yourself up for not being more extroverted or for not meeting societal expectations. Be kind to yourself, recognize your value, and know that your quiet nature is just as important as any other leadership trait.

- **Be present in the moment**: Quiet confidence comes from being fully present, whether you're speaking in front of a group, participating in a meeting, or simply having a conversation. Being mindful of the present moment allows you to respond thoughtfully and calmly, which helps to project confidence.

Real-life example:

- **Warren Buffett**, one of the most successful investors in the world, is known for his quiet confidence and reserved demeanor. Despite his immense wealth and influence, Buffett has always remained humble and grounded. His leadership and investment decisions are guided by careful thought and confidence in his process, not the need for attention or validation.

Conclusion: Embracing Quiet Power

Rewriting the narrative around introversion and reclaiming your quiet confidence is not about becoming someone you are not—it's about embracing who you are and recognizing the strength in your natural tendencies. Introverts bring valuable qualities to the table, including deep thinking, empathy, strategic insight, and authenticity. By reframing the messages you've received and embracing your true self, you can step into your quiet power and lead with confidence, purpose, and grace.

Remember, you don't have to shout to be heard. Your quiet, reflective nature is a strength that, when nurtured, can lead you to success, fulfillment, and personal growth. Embrace your introverted qualities, trust your instincts, and move forward with the quiet confidence that comes from knowing who you truly are.

Chapter 14

Creating Success on Your Terms

Introduction: Reclaiming Success

In society today, success is often measured by external factors: wealth, fame, the size of your following, or the constant hustle to keep up with others. But these traditional metrics of success can feel overwhelming, especially for introverts who thrive on quiet, thoughtful approaches to work and life. It's easy to get caught up in the race to be the loudest, most visible, or most successful in the eyes of others. However, this chapter is dedicated to helping you redefine success on your own terms and build a life and business that reflects your values, desires, and quiet strengths.

For introverts, success doesn't have to look like the loud, bustling world of "hustle culture" or constant visibility. Instead, you can create a version of success that feels authentic, sustainable, and aligned with your inner goals. It's about finding what success means for you, defining your own metrics of success, and moving toward it at your own pace, without the pressure of external expectations.

In this chapter, we'll explore how you can carve out your unique path to success—one that prioritizes authenticity, thoughtfulness, and long-term fulfillment over traditional measures of achievement. We'll look at real-life examples of quiet businesses thriving in niche ways, and discuss how to let go of comparison, visibility pressure, and the need to measure up to others in order to find your true version of success.

1. Defining Your Own Metrics of Success

The Problem with Society's Standard Metrics of Success

In most modern cultures, success is equated with a few key external markers: the size of your bank account, the number of followers you have, or how visible you are in the public eye. These traditional metrics can be particularly stifling for introverts, who tend to focus more on quality over quantity, and value deep work over surface-level achievements. Introverts often feel disconnected from the standard metrics of success, as they may not resonate with their natural inclinations.

For introverts, the first step toward success is to define it on your own terms. What does success look like to you? What values and goals drive you? This may involve asking difficult but important questions, such as:

- **What makes me feel fulfilled and accomplished?**
- **What kind of impact do I want to have in my work and life?**
- **How do I want to spend my time, energy, and resources?**
- **What does happiness look like for me—personally, professionally, and relationally?**

Success may not always be about monetary gain or external validation; it can be about achieving personal fulfillment, creative expression, or creating a lasting impact in a way that feels authentic to you.

Redefining Success as a Personal Journey

For introverts, defining success means shifting the focus from the loud and visible achievements to a more internal, sustainable, and meaningful definition of success. Instead of comparing yourself to others, focus on what truly matters to you and set individual goals based on your own vision and desires.

Some alternative metrics for success might include:

- **Personal growth**: Measuring success through learning, self-improvement, and pushing past your comfort zone.

- **Work-life harmony**: Achieving balance between your personal and professional life, without sacrificing your mental health.

- **Impact**: Creating value that helps others or serves a greater cause, even if it's on a small scale.

- **Creative fulfillment**: Finding joy in the process of creation, whether that's through art, writing, design, or innovation.

- **Peace and contentment**: Defining success by inner peace, contentment with your life, and the ability to navigate challenges with grace.

By defining success in your own terms, you create a roadmap that's uniquely suited to you—one that aligns with your personality, your values, and your strengths.

2. Case Examples of Quiet Businesses Thriving in Niche Ways

Quiet Businesses Making a Big Impact

Many successful businesses today have built their empires by focusing on niche markets, catering to a small but highly dedicated audience. These businesses thrive by providing value, not by trying to reach as many people as possible or by jumping on trends. Instead, they focus on creating quality products or services that resonate deeply with a specific group of people, often quietly and with an understated presence.

Some examples of quiet businesses that have thrived include:

- **The Calm App**: Calm, a meditation and wellness app, found its niche in the wellness market by offering a calm, reflective experience for users looking for relaxation and mental clarity. The app focuses on mindfulness, relaxation, and mental health, tapping into a growing trend of emotional well-being while maintaining a relatively low-key presence in the market.

- **Small Batch Artisanal Businesses**: Many introverted entrepreneurs have built successful small businesses based on craftsmanship and personalization. These businesses often thrive by offering products that are high-quality, thoughtfully designed, and made with a personal touch. For example, a small business that specializes in hand-made furniture or custom jewelry may not have mass-market appeal but can find devoted customers willing to pay a premium for unique, handcrafted goods.

- **Seth Godin's AltMBA**: Seth Godin's AltMBA is an online learning program that operates quietly but consistently in the business and leadership education space. Godin has built a reputation for offering thought-provoking, in-depth content on leadership and creativity, all while maintaining a relatively small, exclusive, and niche audience. His success is not measured by the size of his audience, but by the impact he has on those who engage with his work.

These businesses thrive because they focus on quality, authenticity, and building lasting relationships with a select group of customers. Rather than chasing after mass appeal or trying to compete in a crowded marketplace, they cultivate a niche and create value on their own terms.

The Power of Consistency Over Flashy Visibility

What these businesses have in common is the ability to build trust and loyalty with their audiences over time. Introverts excel in this area because they often prefer to build deep, sustained connections rather than chase short-term wins. Quiet businesses may take longer to build, but the relationships that form along the way are often more meaningful and lasting.

For introverts, focusing on consistent value creation—through content, products, services, or relationships—can lead to greater success in the long run. Visible success may come later, but it's built on a foundation of trust, integrity, and value that resonates with your audience.

3. Letting Go of Comparison and Visibility Pressure

The Dangers of Comparison Culture

One of the biggest challenges for introverts in today's world of hustle culture is the constant pressure to compare themselves to others. In an age where social media showcases only the most visible and flashy successes, it can be easy to feel like you're not doing enough, not achieving enough, or not visible enough. This comparison culture can lead to burnout, frustration, and self-doubt.

Introverts often feel this pressure even more acutely because their natural inclination is to work in a quieter, more focused way. They may compare their behind-the-scenes work to the outward success of others and feel like their efforts aren't enough. However, comparison is the antithesis of quiet power and sustainable success.

Embracing Your Own Pace

To overcome the pressure of comparison, it's essential to embrace your unique journey and focus on your own path to success. While others may choose to rush, hustle, or put themselves in the spotlight, introverts can thrive by slowing down, focusing on their strengths, and staying aligned with their values.

Here are some strategies for letting go of comparison:

- **Focus on your progress**, not the achievements of others. Celebrate the small wins and the steps you're taking toward your own success.

- **Define success on your terms**. Don't let societal standards or the success stories of others define your goals. Set your own markers for success based on what feels right for you.

- **Create boundaries with social media**. Social media often fosters a sense of competition, comparison, and urgency. Take breaks when needed, unfollow accounts that contribute to negative comparisons, and focus on creating meaningful content rather than keeping up with others.

Real-life example:

- **Susan Cain**, the author of *Quiet: The Power of Introverts in a World That Can't Stop Talking*, has become a thought leader in advocating for the strengths of introverts. She has built her success by staying true to her message, not trying to compete with louder voices, and focusing on creating value for introverts everywhere. Cain's success is a testament to how introverts can achieve powerful success by focusing on their own narrative, rather than comparing themselves to extroverted role models.

Conclusion: Crafting Your Own Quiet Success

Success isn't about chasing the spotlight or competing in the loud, crowded marketplace. It's about defining success on your own terms and cultivating a life and business that reflect your authentic self. For introverts, success may look different than it does for extroverts, but it can be just as powerful and impactful. By focusing on creating a niche, building meaningful relationships, and letting go of the pressure to conform to societal expectations, introverts can build a legacy of success that is rooted in authenticity, integrity, and quiet strength.

The key is to embrace your own pace, trust your unique strengths, and remain true to your values. Quiet businesses, quiet success, and quiet leadership are all powerful forces when they are aligned with your true self. When you stop comparing yourself to others and start building on your own terms, you create a business and a life that is authentic, fulfilling, and sustainable for the long term.

Chapter 15

The Quiet Climb Continues

Introduction: The Journey of Quiet Leadership

Throughout this book, we've explored how introverts can thrive in the business world without having to shout for attention or sacrifice their authentic selves. We've seen how introverts, through quiet influence, authenticity, and strategic focus, can lead, build businesses, and succeed without adopting the traditional extroverted norms of success. However, the journey doesn't stop after you've built the foundation of your quiet business empire. The true challenge for introverts in business is sustaining that success, maintaining energy and values over the long term, and evolving in ways that honor their unique leadership style.

In this final chapter, we'll explore how to sustain your energy and business growth while staying true to your core introverted traits. We'll dive into the importance of values-driven growth, the art of evolving your business without losing your identity, and how to create a legacy of silent leadership that impacts others, all while preserving your mental well-being and energy.

This chapter will help you not only continue to climb the ladder of success but to do so on your own terms—quietly, purposefully, and with integrity. By the end of this chapter, you will have practical tools to navigate the ongoing journey of introverted entrepreneurship, ensuring that your growth is both sustainable and in alignment with your true self.

1. Sustaining Your Energy, Values, and Focus Over the Long Term

The Importance of Self-Care for Introverted Entrepreneurs

As an introverted business owner, you've likely experienced the challenges of balancing your personal needs with the demands of running a business. Introverts tend to thrive in quieter, more focused environments, but the pressures of growing a business can push them into spaces of social fatigue, stress, and burnout. Sustaining your energy requires a deep commitment to self-care, recognizing that your energy is a finite resource that needs to be replenished regularly.

The key to sustaining your energy over the long term is creating a self-care plan that includes:

- **Structured recovery time**: Introverts need to recharge after social interactions, meetings, and public-facing tasks. Set aside quiet time in your schedule to rest and reflect, away from the hustle of daily operations. This will help you recharge your mental energy and stay grounded in your business.

- **Physical activity**: Exercise is essential for maintaining energy levels, especially when you spend long hours focused on deep work. Whether it's yoga, walking, or light strength training, regular physical activity helps clear the mind and improve mental clarity, which is essential for long-term success.

- **Boundaries around work and personal life**: Introverts thrive when they have the space to focus on their work in solitude. Setting clear boundaries around work hours and personal time helps prevent overload and ensures that you're not constantly "on" for clients, customers, or collaborators.

Real-life example:

- **Tim Ferriss**, a successful entrepreneur and author, practices self-care by scheduling regular recovery days and sticking to a clear work-life balance. Ferriss emphasizes the importance of down-time and taking deliberate breaks from the busyness of business in order to stay mentally sharp and energized. His approach has allowed him to maintain his energy levels and continue his work without succumbing to burnout.

Staying True to Your Values as You Grow

Sustaining long-term success as an introverted entrepreneur is not just about maintaining your physical energy, but also about staying true to your values. As your business grows and evolves, it's easy to get caught up in the chase for more profits, larger audiences, or broader influence. However, it's crucial to remain anchored in the core values that led you to start your business in the first place. This will keep your growth aligned with your authentic self, preventing you from losing sight of what really matters.

- **Revisit your "why" regularly**: At regular intervals, reflect on why you started your business in the first place. What values did you want to bring into the world? How do you want your work to impact others? By revisiting your "why", you ensure that your growth aligns with your mission and that you're not swayed by external pressures.

- **Honor your introverted nature**: As your business grows, you may be tempted to adopt extroverted strategies to keep up with the competition. However, true success lies in remaining authentic. Honor your need for quiet time, deep focus, and reflection. Don't let the noise of the business world pull you away from the practices that sustain your energy and creativity.

Real-life example:

- **Patagonia**, the outdoor clothing brand, has grown immensely while staying true to its environmental values. The company focuses on producing sustainable products, maintaining fair labor practices, and prioritizing environmental impact over profit maximization. Despite its size, Patagonia has built a brand around its commitment to authentic values rather than chasing market trends. This commitment to values-driven growth has made the company an admired leader in both business and social responsibility.

2. Evolving Your Business While Honoring Your Introversion

Adapting Without Losing Your Authenticity

As your business grows, you'll likely face decisions that require evolution—new products, expanding teams, shifting business models, or branching into new markets. For introverts, the challenge lies in growing the business without sacrificing their authenticity or compromising their workstyle. It's easy to feel pressure to follow industry trends, adopt aggressive marketing tactics, or make choices that aren't in line with your values just to compete in the marketplace.

However, the key to long-term success is evolving your business in a way that honors your introverted strengths. This means finding innovative ways to grow while maintaining the focus, introspection, and authenticity that made your business successful in the first place. It's about strategically choosing what to embrace and what to discard as you evolve.

Some strategies for evolving your business while honoring your introversion:

- **Slow, strategic growth**: Instead of opting for rapid growth, focus on scaling your business in a way that feels sustainable and manageable. Slow, intentional growth allows you to maintain control over the direction of your business and ensures that you're not overwhelmed by the demands of expansion.

- **Delegate or automate tasks**: Introverts excel in deep, focused work, but can often feel drained by tasks that require constant interaction or attention to detail. Delegating tasks like customer service, social media management, or day-to-day operations can free up time and mental space to focus on the work that matters most.

- **Build a team that complements your strengths**: As your business expands, surround yourself with people who share your values but complement your introverted strengths. This could mean hiring extroverts who excel in areas like networking, client relations, and sales, allowing you to focus on areas where you excel, like strategy, writing, or content creation.

Real-life example:

- Apple, under Steve Jobs' leadership, built a technology empire while staying true to its values of design and innovation. Jobs was known for his quiet, focused leadership and for maintaining control over key elements of the business while allowing his team to take on leadership roles in other areas. This allowed Apple to evolve and grow without losing its core identity. Jobs' ability to adapt while staying authentic is a prime example of how introverted leaders can evolve their businesses without compromising their values.

3. The Legacy of Silent Leadership

Building a Legacy Through Quiet Leadership

The true power of introverted leadership lies in its ability to create a lasting legacy that reflects values, vision, and authenticity. A strong legacy isn't necessarily about achieving fame or accumulating wealth; it's about impact—how your work influences others and creates positive change in the world. As an introvert, you have the ability to build a legacy of quiet leadership that leaves a lasting mark without needing to constantly be in the spotlight.

A legacy of quiet leadership is built on:

- **Consistency**: Introverts often thrive in consistent, deliberate action. A legacy is built over time, through thoughtful contributions and sustained efforts.

- **Authenticity**: True leaders leave a legacy by being true to themselves, not by conforming to external pressures. Your authenticity will inspire others to trust you and follow your example.

- **Empathy and service**: Quiet leaders often lead by serving others. A legacy of service, grounded in **empathy**, creates a ripple effect that inspires others to do the same.

How to Build a Legacy of Silent Leadership

- **Mentorship and community impact**: Introverts often excel in one-on-one mentorship, deep conversations, and personal connections. Building a legacy of quiet leadership can involve mentoring the next generation, guiding others in your field, and giving back to the community through volunteer work or charity initiatives.

- **Share your wisdom**: Introverts may not always seek the limelight, but sharing your knowledge and insights—whether through writing, speaking, or teaching—can leave a lasting legacy. Creating content that reflects your expertise allows your influence to grow and reach others, even when you're not in the room.

- **Focus on long-term impact**: Introverts are often more focused on long-term growth and lasting change than short-term wins. Building a legacy involves thinking about the future—how your work will continue to impact others long after you're gone.

Real-life example:

- Maya Angelou, the renowned poet and civil rights activist, left a powerful legacy of quiet leadership through her written work and speeches. While she was not a typical "loud" leader, her influence and impact on social justice, literature, and human rights are undeniable. Angelou's quiet strength, empathy, and wisdom continue to inspire generations, proving that introverts can leave an incredible legacy without needing to be loud or constantly visible.

Conclusion: Quietly Climbing to Lasting Success

The climb to success is not a sprint; it is a journey that requires patience, intention, and alignment with your core values. As an introverted entrepreneur, you have the unique ability to build success quietly, without sacrificing your energy or authenticity. By sustaining your energy, evolving your business thoughtfully, and focusing on the legacy of your leadership, you can create a lasting impact that reflects your true self.

Quiet leadership is powerful because it is authentic, consistent, and deeply rooted in values. The quiet climb doesn't require grand gestures or attention-seeking behavior; it's about making steady progress, honoring your own pace, and building relationships that foster long-term trust and impact. The legacy of quiet leadership is one of deep influence, meaningful connection, and lasting change—crafted not by loud proclamations, but by the power of quiet, focused intention.

Epilogue

The Quiet Climb – Leading with Purpose, Power, and Authenticity

Throughout this book, we've explored how introverts can not only thrive in business but also lead with power, authenticity, and a quiet strength that speaks volumes. From redefining the narrative around introversion to building success on your terms, we've seen how introverted entrepreneurs have the unique ability to create sustainable businesses that align with their values, strengths, and vision. The journey of introverted leadership is not about conforming to external expectations or competing for attention; it's about cultivating a path that is uniquely yours—one that allows you to embrace your introverted traits while achieving long-term success.

The quiet climb is a journey that is deeply rooted in authenticity, intentionality, and sustainable growth. This approach stands in stark contrast to the loud hustle culture that often values visibility and flashiness over depth and substance. As we have explored, introverts are perfectly equipped to build businesses and lead teams in ways that are grounded in thoughtful reflection, empathy, and clear focus. Quiet leadership is not a passive experience; it's an active commitment to creating value, fostering deep relationships, and leaving a legacy that reflects your true self.

One of the key takeaways from this book is that success doesn't have to look like what society tells us it should. There is no need to follow the traditional markers of wealth, fame, or visibility. Instead, introverts can define success on their own terms—focusing on meaningful work, personal fulfillment, and the impact they want to create in the world. This new narrative allows introverts to flourish without sacrificing their energy, values, or unique way of contributing to the world.

From building authentic relationships and nurturing a quiet community to embracing strategic partnerships that align with your strengths, introverts can excel by focusing on quality over quantity. The key is to stay true to your vision and avoid getting caught up in the pressure to conform to the expectations of others. Whether you're navigating the pressures of collaboration, branding, or sales, the quiet power of introverted leadership offers a distinct advantage—one that doesn't require performing, shouting, or pretending to be someone you're not.

As we explored in Chapter 15, sustaining success is an ongoing process. Introverts have the unique ability to approach growth at a steady pace, ensuring that their businesses are not only scalable but sustainable. By prioritizing energy management, setting clear boundaries, and focusing on the things that truly matter, introverts can maintain a thriving business without burning out. Growth doesn't have to come at the expense of your authentic self; instead, it can align with your core values and lead to a legacy of quiet leadership.

This journey also emphasizes the importance of self-reflection and knowing when to pivot or recalibrate. Just because a certain path is popular or well-traveled doesn't mean it's the right path for you. As an introverted entrepreneur, learning to say no to opportunities that don't align with your goals or energy is one of the most powerful ways to preserve your focus and maintain a sustainable work-life balance.

Legacy—the final theme in this book—comes not from the noise you make but from the impact you leave behind. By leading with integrity, focusing on long-term relationships, and staying aligned with your inner vision, you can create a legacy that lasts far beyond your business. Introverts often make the most authentic, respected leaders precisely because their leadership is based on substance, empathy, and a deep commitment to their vision. This type of legacy is felt by those who work with you, collaborate with you, and benefit from your products or services.

In the end, the quiet climb is about more than building a business—it's about creating a life that reflects your values, allows you to contribute in a way that is true to yourself, and leaves a lasting impact. It's about finding joy in the journey, not just the destination. Introverts don't need to be louder to be heard—they need to be authentic, intentional, and persistent in their approach.

The journey of quiet leadership is not easy, but it is one that leads to profound fulfillment, personal growth, and long-lasting success. Embrace your introverted strengths, stay focused on your vision, and continue the quiet climb with confidence, purpose, and resilience. The world needs your voice, your ideas, and your leadership—on your terms, at your pace, and in your own quiet, powerful way.

www.ingramcontent.com/pod-product-compliance
Lightning Source LLC
Chambersburg PA
CBHW071421210326
41597CB00020B/3599